IMAGES
of America

CLEVELAND HEIGHTS CONGREGATIONS

On the cover: **FIRST COMMUNION AT ST. LOUIS CHURCH, 1951**. Proud parents captured on camera this important event in their children's religious lives. This Roman Catholic parish was established in Cleveland Heights in 1947 and built a church, a school, and a convent for the nuns who taught at the school. The school closed in 2007, and like Catholic parishes around the country, St. Louis Church will merge with another parish. (St. Louis Church.)

IMAGES
of America

CLEVELAND HEIGHTS CONGREGATIONS

Marian J. Morton

ARCADIA
PUBLISHING

ISBN 978-0-7385-6142-4

Published by Arcadia Publishing
Charleston SC, Chicago IL, Portsmouth NH, San Francisco CA

Printed in the United States of America

Library of Congress Catalog Card Number: 2008932671

For all general information contact Arcadia Publishing at:
Telephone 843-853-2070
Fax 843-853-0044
E-mail sales@arcadiapublishing.com
For customer service and orders:
Toll-Free 1-888-313-2665

Visit us on the Internet at www.arcadiapublishing.com

Contents

ACKNOWLEDGMENTS

I want to thank all the kind, generous, knowledgeable people who helped me write this book, including Fran Bayless (Fairmount Presbyterian Church); Chris Tapei Fay (Forest Hill Church); Carol Phillips (Noble Road Presbyterian Church); Sylvia Robinson (New Spirit Revival Center); Kathryn Klaber (Church of the Redeemer United Methodist); Demo Solaru and Angela Lawson (Cedar Hill Baptist Church); Bob Cheshier (St. Paul's Episcopal Church); Rev. Gary Mitchener (St. Alban Episcopal Church); Virginia Krumholz and Don Shepherd (Episcopal Diocese of Ohio); Chris Krosel (Cleveland Catholic Diocese); Diane Pexa and Tim Ryan (St. Louis Church); Rev. Don King (Hope Lutheran Church); Rev. Robert Hanson (First English and Bethlehem Lutheran Church); Rev. Amy Campbell (Disciples Christian Church); Darlene Hawkins (Church of Christ at Forest Hill); Ellen Petler (Park Synagogue); Laura Gooch (Beth El-The Heights Synagogue); Eleanor Richardson (Church of the Saviour); Kia Wolf (Cleveland Heights Community Relations Department); Cyndy Bernheimer (First Church of Christ, Scientist, Cleveland); AnneMarie M. Grassi (Open Doors); Kathryn Lad (Home Repair Resource Center); Daisy Jackson (Greater Peace Missionary Baptist Church); Dr. Judith Cetina (St. Ann Church); Sid Pryor (Grace Lutheran Church); Miriam Klein (Oheb Zedek-Taylor Road Synagogue); Hazel Haffner (Heights Emergency Food Center); Suzanne Tonsing (SS. Constantine and Helen Greek Orthodox Cathedral); Dawn Dumm (Bethel Church of Cleveland Heights); Florence Chase (Church of the Master); Eric Silverman (Cleveland Heights High School Alumni Foundation); Janice Kalman (Nottingham Spirk and Design); Sabine Kretzschmar (Shaker Historical Society); James Garrett for his wonderful photographs; Ken Goldberg for his expert advice on architecture; John Carroll University for financial support; the Cleveland Heights Historical Society for the invitation that initiated this book; Kay Heylman for correcting some of my mistakes; and most of all, Kara Hamley O'Donnell, historic preservation planner for the City of Cleveland Heights, who helps all of us know and appreciate our city.

The author's proceeds from this book will be donated to the Heights Emergency Food Center founded by the Heights Interfaith Council.

INTRODUCTION

Since 1875, dozens of religious congregations have made their homes in Cleveland Heights. In the intervening years, these congregations have been shaped by world events, including two world wars, the Holocaust, the creation of the state of Israel and the Second Vatican Council, and by national trends. These include the arrival of millions of immigrants from Europe, many of them Catholic or Jewish; the Protestant crusade to evangelize the American city and countryside (as well as the Far East) in the last decades of the 19th century; the migration from the cities to the suburbs from the 1890s to the present; the renewed interest of Protestants, Catholics, and Jews in organized religion in the post–World War II period; the social activism that began in the 1960s with the civil rights movement; and beginning in the 1970s, the relative decline of some mainline Protestant denominations.

Cleveland Heights congregations have in turn shaped the lives of their members, most importantly serving their spiritual needs, providing joy, enlightenment, and solace. Religious rituals have commemorated life's important events, including baptism, first communion, bar and bat mitzvah, confirmation, marriage, and death.

Congregations have also served the larger community. They have been welcomed by city officials, developers, and most—if not all—neighbors and neighboring congregations. The public importance of religious congregations has been acknowledged by their frequent use of public schools for worship services.

In 1875, when the first congregation, the Fairmount Methodist Episcopal Church, celebrated its first service in the Superior Schoolhouse, this southeastern corner of East Cleveland Township was called "Heathen Heights" or "Heathen Ridge." Established Methodist, Presbyterian, and Evangelical churches in Cleveland and East Cleveland founded small mission churches to convert the neighborhood's farmers, quarry owners, and their laborers. These country churches became social centers of the community and attracted new residents to this isolated rural village.

Where the missionaries led, suburban real estate developers followed. Less interested in saving souls than in making money, entrepreneurs like Patrick Calhoun and Oris P. and Mantis J. Van Sweringen realized that churches, like streetcars, attracted residents; they encouraged the building of both. Cleveland Heights grew from a village of 1,056 in 1901, when it became independent of East Cleveland Township, to a city of 50,945 in 1930. Protestant churches kept pace. Some built ambitious Gothic Revival churches that reflected their new membership and new affluence in this prosperous, elite suburb. In 1915, the first Catholic congregation, St. Ann, the creation of priest-developer Fr. John Mary Powers, challenged Protestant hegemony. Another Catholic church, two Catholic schools, a Catholic convent, and a Catholic college followed.

Jewish institutions followed also. The first was Mayfield Cemetery, established in 1890 by two Reform Jewish congregations. Neither settled in Cleveland Heights. From the 1920s through the 1950s, Conservative and Orthodox congregations built temples and synagogues there. Jewish shops clustered along Coventry Road, Jewish schools, shops, and social service agencies along Taylor Road. These helped to maintain Jewish ethnic and religious identity, but they also generated tensions within the suburb as it made an uneasy transition to religious pluralism.

These tensions surfaced especially during the 1920s and again during and after World War II when religiously affiliated institutions moved, or tried to move, into some of the suburb's great mansions. The Depression and World War II made these homes, symbols of the suburb's earlier elitist aspirations, too expensive or too unfashionable for their original owners to maintain. Their sale to Protestant, Catholic, or Jewish institutions seemed a good solution, except to neighbors. These transformations altered the once-exclusive residential neighborhoods and the city itself.

In 1960, the Cleveland Heights population peaked at 61,813. New congregations built new houses of worship, and older congregations built new additions. The Colonial Revival style, popular in public buildings, private homes, and churches, looked back to the past, but the reality was that the suburb had become a different place. Its population and its congregations now included people of all creeds, ethnic groups, and classes.

Cleveland Heights continued to change. Beginning in the 1960s, the suburb's population declined and became multiracial and less wealthy. Protestant and Catholic congregations helped to ease the racial transition by welcoming nonwhite members, and Protestant, Catholic, and Jewish congregations led the efforts to sustain a racially integrated community. An interfaith council fed the needy.

Some Protestant and Jewish congregations have left Cleveland Heights; their houses of worship have found new uses, both sacred and secular. Two Catholic churches will merge. Other congregations have stayed to serve the community's changing needs. They host classes, concerts, lectures, and support groups of all kinds for adults, and preschools, day care, and after-school programs for children, along with a wide variety of other civic functions. Congregations have newly welcomed women pastors. New congregations have joined the community, and like the very first congregations, these often share or borrow worship space, seeking new members for themselves and the community.

Over the last century and a quarter, Cleveland Heights congregations have continued to play their primary spiritual role. But churches, temples, and synagogues have also encouraged the suburb's growth, sustaining and sometimes changing its neighborhoods. Their houses of worship, ranging from modest storefronts to stately cathedrals, have enriched the city's landscape; their spires, turrets, and domes have enlivened its skyline. Their calls to action have aroused the community's conscience. Religious pluralism has nurtured religious, ethnic, economic, and racial diversity, as well as controversy and conflict. Religious congregations, in short, have helped to sustain the vitality of Cleveland Heights.

One

Country Churches 1875–1920

In the decades following the Civil War, mainline Protestant denominations, anxious to close wartime rifts and reclaim their central place in American life, set out to "evangelize the world in this generation," to use the phrase of revivalist Dwight L. Moody. To achieve this, they sent missionaries around the globe, into urban neighborhoods now congested with Catholic and Jewish immigrants, and even into the American countryside.

Four Cleveland Heights congregations illustrate this ambitious goal: the Fairmount/Heights Methodist Episcopal Church (now Church of the Saviour); Cleveland Heights Presbyterian Church (now Forest Hill Church); the Noble Road Bible Chapel (now Noble Road Presbyterian Church), and the Cleveland Heights Evangelical Mission (now Church of the Redeemer United Methodist). All were founded as mission churches. The term *mission* referred to their errand into "Heathen Heights" to gain new adherents and to their financial and other dependence on more established churches. To a 19th-century Protestant, the term *heathen* probably meant anyone who did not belong to one's own particular Protestant church.

These pioneer congregations worshipped initially in borrowed or shared spaces until they could afford to build their own churches. These were modest frame structures compatible with nearby homes and the surrounding countryside. Two congregations—then called Fairmount (later Heights) Methodist Episcopal Church and Cleveland Heights Presbyterian Church—built close to the village's equally modest city hall and public schools in suburban allotments that grew up around them. The other two—the Noble Road Bible Chapel and the Cleveland Heights Evangelical Mission—were located in more distant neighborhoods that remained rural even in the second decade of the 20th century.

All four congregations encountered the challenges of life in this rural village, including sparsely settled neighborhoods, financial hardships, relative isolation from parent congregations, shared pastors, and the rigors of rural transportation. On the other hand, their members often included the community's prominent families, and their churches became centers of community social life and civic action. These congregations constituted the vanguard of suburban settlement. Proselytizing not only for themselves but also for the larger community, they helped to transform the country village into a thriving suburb.

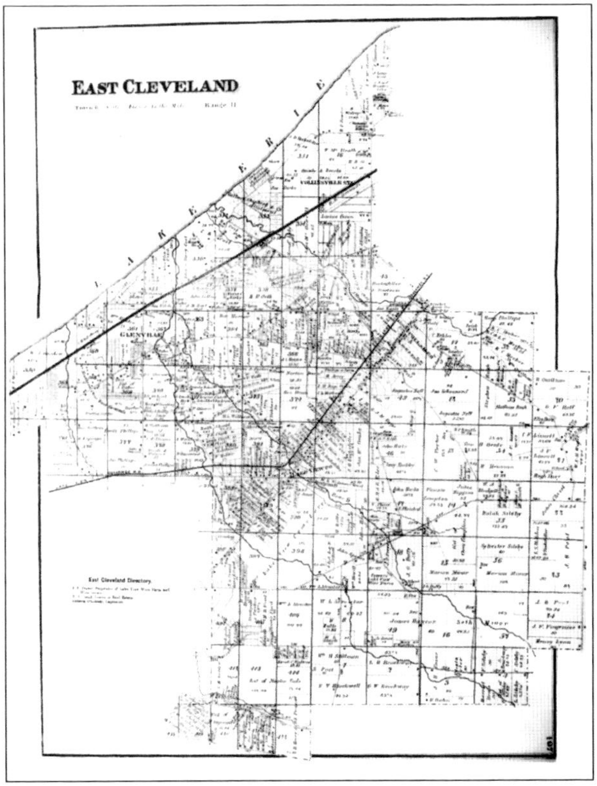

EAST CLEVELAND TOWNSHIP, 1874. The township included the area that became Cleveland Heights. This atlas locates the two schoolhouses (one on Superior Road and one on Noble Road) that became the first worship sites for Fairmount Methodist Church and the Noble Road Bible Chapel. It also identifies the farms, orchards, and vineyards of families like the Preyers, Silsbys, and Minors, who became church founders and members. (Western Reserve Historical Society.)

HAYCOX FARM AND QUARRY, 1874. The atlas also included these idealized pictures of the properties of James Haycox. The stone quarry was located where Cain Park is now; his farm and home were to the west on Lee Road. The 1880 census describes Haycox as a farmer, born in 1824 in England. He later enjoyed considerable financial success as a developer. Haycox was also a member of Fairmount Methodist Episcopal Church, whose first two sites were just to the north of his property. (Western Reserve Historical Society.)

SUPERIOR SCHOOLHOUSE, C. 1894. Fairmount Methodist Episcopal Church met first in this small public schoolhouse. According to the congregation's history, the neighborhood was called Heathen Heights because of the "weekend 'celebrations' of the stone quarry workers," probably in Haycox's quarry. According to one observer, the visiting preacher "used to tell about Hell and how hard it was not to go there." The pupils seen here may or may not have been Methodists. (City of Cleveland Heights.)

FAIRMOUNT METHODIST EPISCOPAL CHURCH. Just to the south of the schoolhouse, members of the congregation built this modest Gothic church in 1878. Only the pointed arch over the doorway indicates that this is a church. One member, years later, recalled that the midweek prayer meeting was "a time for all the boys to congregate in the backseats and giggle and laugh." *Fairmount* refers to the post office located in the general store at Mayfield and Superior Roads. (Church of the Saviour.)

HEIGHTS METHODIST EPISCOPAL CHURCH. In 1904, the congregation had outgrown its first two homes, changed its name, and moved south on Superior Road to this wood-frame Gothic Revival building designed by architect Sidney R. Badgley. One member remembered, "the entire neighborhood comprised the congregation of the old Methodist church, then the only church upon the Heights," and the center of the small community's social life. (Church of the Saviour.)

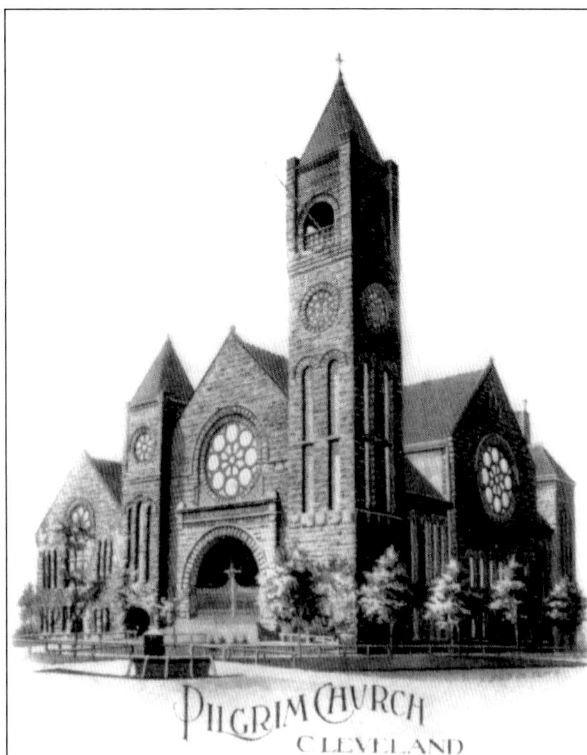

PILGRIM CONGREGATIONAL CHURCH. Badgley also designed this building, now Pilgrim United Church of Christ, completed in 1890. Although Pilgrim is much larger and built of rough stone, both churches have asymmetrical facades with one dominant tower. Both interiors are organized on the Akron plan, with seating that fans out in a semicircle from the pulpit. Badgley also designed the third home of Cleveland Heights Presbyterian Church at Mayfield and Preyer Roads. (Special Collections, Cleveland State University.)

Haycox Window. Dedicated to the memory of James Haycox, this is one of several lovely stained-glass windows that still illuminate the simple interior of the original Heights Methodist Episcopal Church, now the home of Christ Our Redeemer African Methodist Episcopal Church and the oldest standing religious structure in Cleveland Heights. Haycox died in 1903 and is buried in Lake View Cemetery. (City of Cleveland Heights.)

Gooding Organ. This organ was dedicated to the memory of Fannie Haycox Gooding, who died in 1908. She was the daughter of William Haycox, the older brother of James. Fannie married her neighbor, Charles Gooding, and both were members of this Methodist church. Gooding was also the first elected treasurer of the village and sold the village the property for Lee School. (City of Cleveland Heights.)

LADIES AID SOCIETY OF THE HEIGHTS METHODIST EPISCOPAL CHURCH, 1910. Although very few Protestant denominations ordained women, they have constituted the majority of Protestant church members at least since the 19th century. Churches did provide women with a rare opportunity to play important public roles as they left their homes to raise funds and proselytize for their congregations. This Methodist group welcomed all women in the neighborhood, regardless of their denomination. This horse and buggy was the fastest way to travel on Cleveland Heights' dirt roads in the congregation's early years. The Ladies Aid Society remained active, raising the monies for the kitchen and dining room of the church when the congregation, then Church of the Saviour, moved to Bradford and Lee Roads. (Church of the Saviour.)

MARCUS M. BROWN HOUSE, C. 1900. Marcus M. Brown developed the Mayfield Heights allotment, bounded by Euclid Heights Boulevard and Superior, Hampshire, and Cadwell Roads. This home is at Euclid Heights Boulevard and Wilton Road. Brown lost financial control of the allotment in 1908 and died in 1909. Although not an active church member, he is said to have given an occasional sermon at the Methodist church that helped anchor and promote his allotment. (Western Reserve Historical Society.)

HARVESTING OATS IN MAYFIELD HEIGHTS. This postcard dates from the first decade of the 20th century and captures the rural flavor of Brown's allotment when the first two Protestant churches were established there. (Special Collections, Cleveland State University.)

O. A. Dean Home and Dairy. O. A. Dean was a founding member of the Methodist congregation and lived nearby on Mayfield Road. Other founding members, also substantial property owners, included James Haycox, Charles Gooding, Seth Minor, Mrs. John Spence, and Mr. and Mrs. Frederick Silsby. (City of Cleveland Heights.)

Lee School. Just to the east of the Superior Schoolhouse and close to the Methodist and Presbyterian churches, Lee School served from 1902 to 1912 as both an elementary and a high school. The substantial brick building had few decorative details other than the rooftop cupola and a broad arched doorway. After the completion of Boulevard School in 1924, Lee School became the district's administration building. It was demolished in 1964. (Cleveland Heights High School Alumni Foundation.)

BECKWITH MEMORIAL CHURCH. The pastor of this church, Rev. A. J. Alexander, is credited with inspiring the founding of Cleveland Heights' first Presbyterian congregation, a mission church initially referred to by the parent congregation as the Mayfield Heights Branch of Beckwith and then Cleveland Heights Presbyterian Church. Beckwith was located at East 107th Street and Deering Avenue before it merged in 1906 with another congregation to form Euclid Avenue Presbyterian Church, which in turn merged to become the Church of the Covenant. (Special Collections, Cleveland State University.)

FIRST MEETING PLACE OF CLEVELAND HEIGHTS PRESBYTERIAN CHURCH. The first few members raised $200 for the expenses of the first year and met here at a member's home on Radnor (then Florence) Road from 1903 to 1906 when they moved to the Superior Schoolhouse, just vacated by the Methodists. One church member described this unpromising scenario for the fledgling church: "Sidewalks were few and far between, mud everywhere, street lights none, families were few . . . Church-going was not the popular thing on Sundays . . . [I]t was not such an inviting field." (Author's collection.)

HELWIG HOUSE ON SUPERIOR ROAD, C. 1882. This photograph of muddy streets, nonexistent sidewalks and streetlights, and a solitary house and barn bears out the rather discouraging picture of the prospects of the new Presbyterian church. The home of Mary Preyer Helwig, the daughter of J. M. Preyer, owner of Lake View Wine Farm and much of the nearby property, was just to the north of the schoolhouse. (City of Cleveland Heights.)

EMIL C. PREYER HOUSE. Emil C. Preyer, the son of J. M. Preyer and a member of the Presbyterian church, sold the growing congregation the property for the first building of its own. The church was located down the street from this house at the northern end of Alvin Road (now Preyer Road) that he was developing. With financial help from its mother church, the congregation raised $15,000 for its building. (James W. Garrett IV.)

CLEVELAND HEIGHTS PRESBYTERIAN CHURCH. The congregation moved in 1908 to this new location at Mayfield and Alvin (Preyer) Roads, seen in the top center of this 1926 Sanborn map. Across Mayfield Road at Superior Road was the city hall. Longtime mayor Frank Cain belonged to this congregation, which also organized the Men's Civic Club of Cleveland Heights, advocates for a public park system. See page 59 for the building in the 1950s. (http://dmc.ohiolink.edu.)

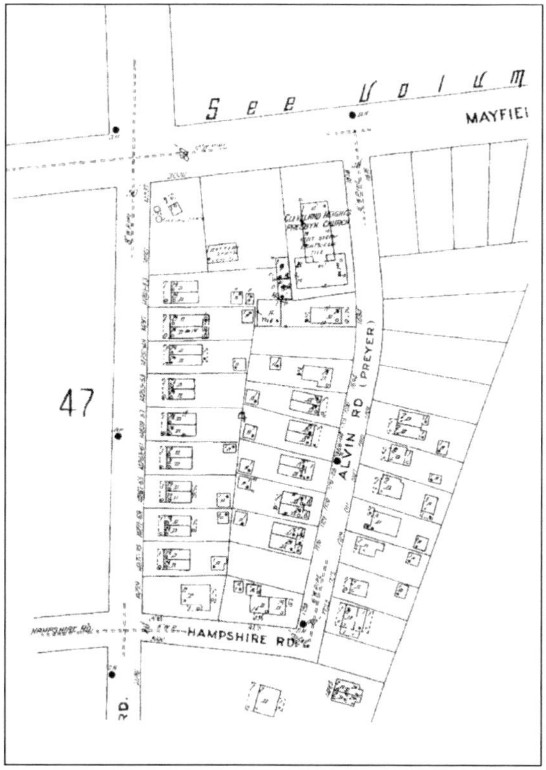

CLEVELAND HEIGHTS' FIRST CITY HALL. Like the Methodists and the Presbyterians, the elected officials of the village of Cleveland Heights met initially in the Superior Schoolhouse before the completion of this small but dignified building near Superior and Mayfield Roads in 1909, a short walk to the Methodist and Presbyterian churches. (City of Cleveland Heights.)

FIRST PRESBYTERIAN CHURCH OF EAST CLEVELAND. This Presbyterian church, perhaps the oldest in the Western Reserve, was founded in 1807 at the site on Euclid Avenue where it is still located. The congregation celebrated its centennial by establishing a mission church, Noble Road Bible Chapel, two miles to the south on Noble Road in Cleveland Heights. (Special Collections, Cleveland State University.)

NOBLE SCHOOLHOUSE. Like the earlier Methodists and Presbyterians, this congregation could not yet afford its own building and met first in this one-story stone schoolhouse. When the schoolhouse was torn down in 1909, the congregation held services in a tent until its first building was finished. "The young church drew most of its members from the immediate neighborhood . . . [S]ome rode to church in horse-drawn buggies," according to the church history. (Noble Road Presbyterian Church.)

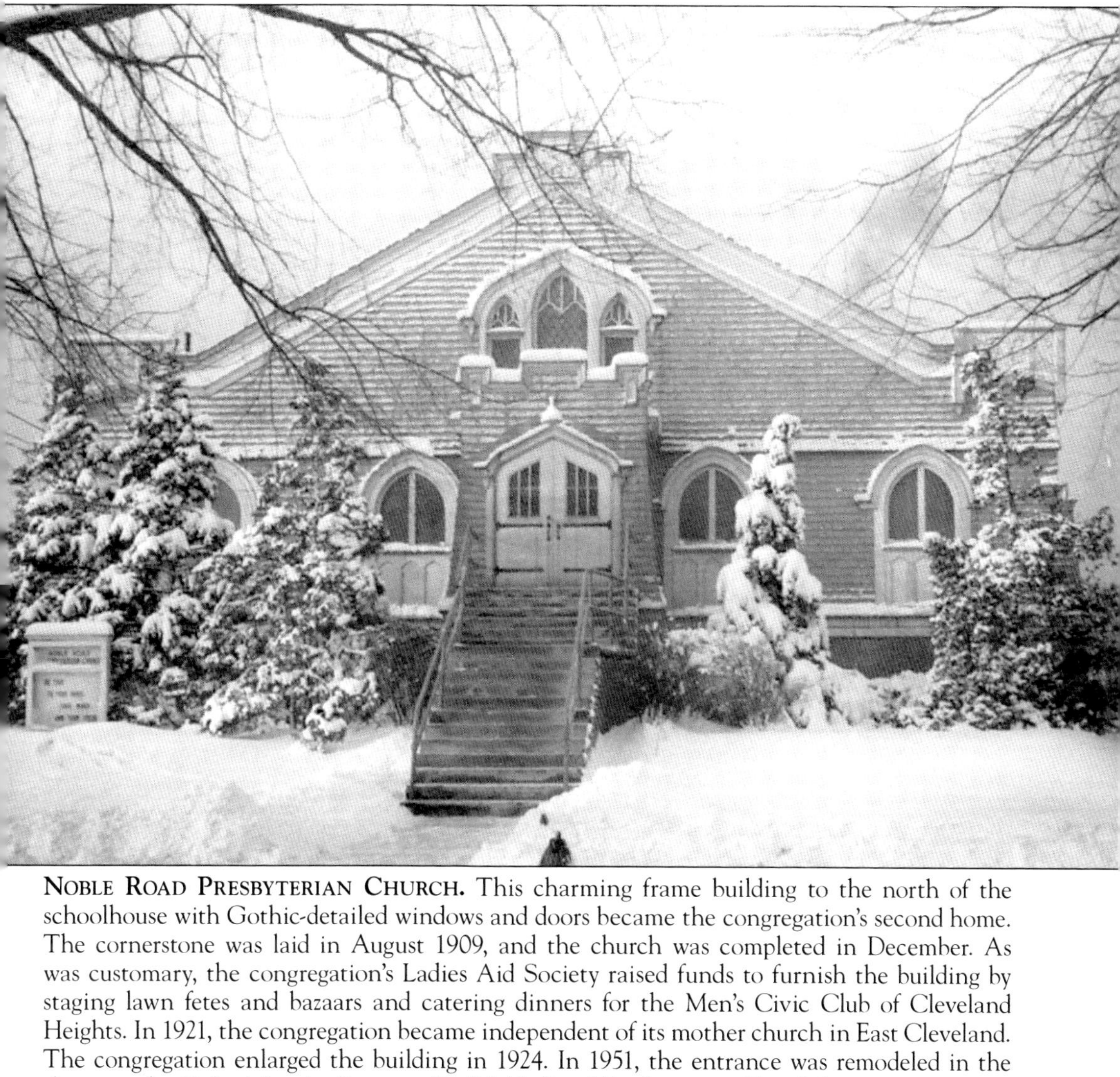

Noble Road Presbyterian Church. This charming frame building to the north of the schoolhouse with Gothic-detailed windows and doors became the congregation's second home. The cornerstone was laid in August 1909, and the church was completed in December. As was customary, the congregation's Ladies Aid Society raised funds to furnish the building by staging lawn fetes and bazaars and catering dinners for the Men's Civic Club of Cleveland Heights. In 1921, the congregation became independent of its mother church in East Cleveland. The congregation enlarged the building in 1924. In 1951, the entrance was remodeled in the then-popular Colonial style. See page 87. (Noble Road Presbyterian Church.)

BLUESTONE FARMHOUSES. Close to the Noble Road Presbyterian Church, these simple homes and barn are reminders of the rural beginnings of the northeast section of Cleveland Heights. Distant from the Mayfield and Superior Roads town center, this mission church served the farmers, dairymen, and quarry workers of the rural neighborhood. (City of Cleveland Heights.)

FAIRMOUNT BOULEVARD FARMHOUSE. In 1853, the Penty family built this Greek Revival farmhouse in what was then rural Warrensville Township. From 1907 until its annexation by Cleveland Heights in 1914, this neighborhood was known as Idlewood, and although streets had been laid out, the neighborhood remained sparsely inhabited until the second decade of the 20th century. (Author's collection.)

Cleveland Heights Evangelical Mission, c. 1920. The last of the early mission churches, this offshoot of a German-speaking Evangelical congregation in Cleveland moved to the southeastern section of Cleveland Heights in 1920. The congregation's first house of worship at the corner of South Taylor and East Scarborough Roads doubled as the home for the minister and his family. (Church of the Redeemer United Methodist.)

East Scarborough and Taylor Roads. The simple church and home fit easily into its neighborhood, which, by 1920, was partially developed. The unpaved streets and the front-facing gabled homes were reminiscent of the recent rural past of this neighborhood. In 1924, this original building became the parsonage when the congregation added a more imposing wooden structure to the original building. (Church of the Redeemer United Methodist.)

CHURCH OF THE REDEEMER UNITED METHODIST. This later photograph shows the 1924 wooden building that remained part of the congregation's home until the 1980s. After merging with two other Evangelical congregations, this congregation adopted the name Church of the Redeemer in 1942. In 1946, the Evangelical Association merged with the Church of the Brethren to form the Evangelical United Brethren Church, and in 1968, when this body merged with the Methodist Church to form the United Methodist Church, the Church of the Redeemer joined the United Methodist denomination. In 1950, the building was remodeled in this Colonial Revival style that became popular in the post–World War II period. (City of Cleveland Heights.)

Two

GOTHIC REVIVALS 1903–1928

During the first three decades of the 20th century, Americans moved from cities to suburbs, taking their churches with them, and vice versa. The outward migration that the streetcar began in the 1890s was accelerated by the automobile through the 1920s, as hopeful suburbanites and congregations pursued fresh air, large tree-shaded lots, green grass, and social status.

The country village of "Heathen Heights" became a rapidly growing, affluent suburb. In 1927, the *Heights Dispatch* boasted that Cleveland Heights was a "city of churches," heralding the arrival of a second generation of Cleveland Heights congregations. These included St. Alban Episcopal Church, Fairmount Presbyterian Church, St. Ann Church (Roman Catholic), St. Martin's Chapel (Episcopal), Heights United Presbyterian Church, Grace Lutheran Church, the new Church of the Saviour (formerly Heights Methodist Church), Trinity Congregational Church, and St. Paul's Episcopal Church. Church news—hours of worship service, sermon titles, meetings of church clubs and groups—shared the *Heights Dispatch*'s front page with real estate news, the number of building permits issued, and new allotments proposed. Suburban worship and suburban growth were clearly linked in the community's mind.

Although two earlier developers, Marcus M. Brown and Emil C. Preyer, cultivated the churches in their allotments, the fortunes of these later congregations were even more intimately linked to developers like Patrick Calhoun, the Van Sweringens, B. R. Deming, and priest-developer Fr. John Mary Powers. All believed that churches enhanced property values. Calhoun, the Van Sweringens, and Powers also proselytized for the extension of streetcars up the suburb's main thoroughfares, correctly assuming that public transportation would guarantee the success of both the real estate and the churches.

Most congregations built—or hoped to build—grand Gothic Revival churches that would add beauty and dignity to new neighborhoods and whose spires and arches would establish a forceful Christian presence. Like the public buildings and private homes of this period, churches expressed the spiritual and secular aspirations of their worshipers and Cleveland Heights.

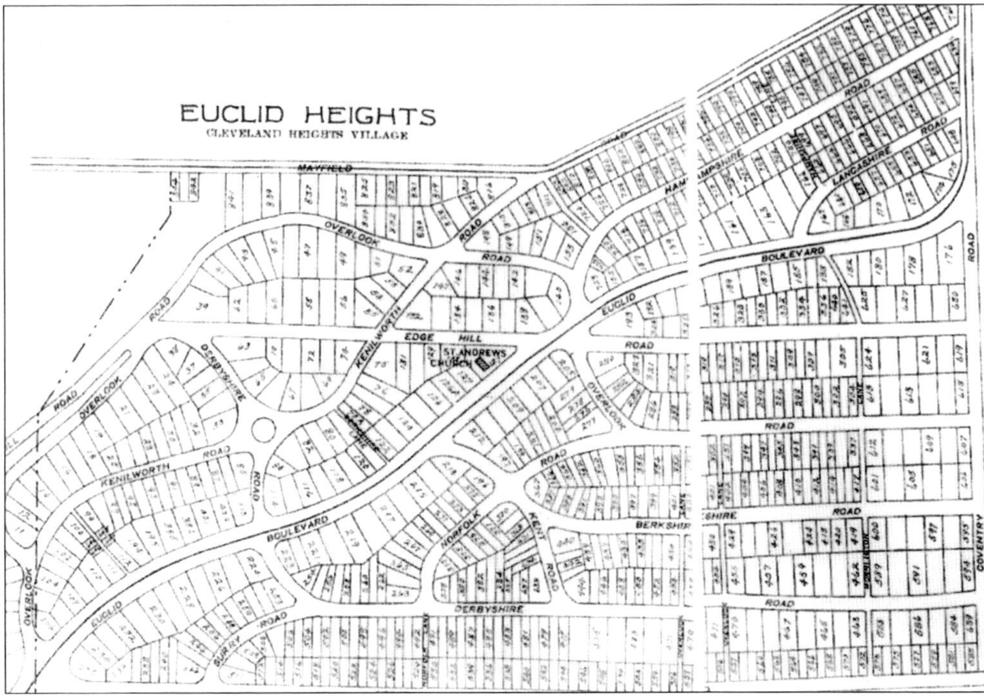

ST. ANDREW'S CHURCH IN THE EUCLID HEIGHTS ALLOTMENT, 1903. St. Andrew's-in-the East, located at the intersection of Edgehill Road and Euclid Heights Boulevard, was the original name of the Episcopalian congregation that became St. Alban Episcopal Church. Calhoun donated the property at this prominent intersection. (Cuyahoga County Archives.)

PATRICK CALHOUN'S EDGEHILL HOME. Patrick Calhoun lived down the street from the church, although he does not appear to have been a member of the congregation. The church was one of Calhoun's several efforts to attract buyers to his allotment. Others included running the streetcar tracks up Cedar Hill and Euclid Heights Boulevard and building the Euclid Club for golf enthusiasts. (Western Reserve Historical Society.)

St. Alban Episcopal Church. This modest Gothic Revival church was brought up the hill from its original location at Murray Hill Road and Fairview Avenue in Little Italy in 1901; this makes St. Alban the second-oldest congregation in Cleveland Heights. Its sponsorship by entrepreneur Calhoun, however, differentiates it from congregations like the early Methodists and Presbyterians, whose sponsors were other churches. St. Alban did receive financial assistance from St. Paul's Episcopal Church, then on Euclid Avenue. (City of Cleveland Heights.)

Wedding at St. Alban Episcopal Church, c. 1936. This wedding photograph captures the intimate interior of the small sanctuary with its distinctive timbered ceiling and elaborate carved woodwork. From 1912 to 1917, the rector of St. Paul's Episcopal Church, Rev. Walter Russell Breed, also assumed the rectorship of St. Alban. (Western Reserve Historical Society.)

PROCESSION AT ST. ALBAN EPISCOPAL CHURCH, 1942. This service celebrated those members of the congregation who served in World War II. Congregations of all denominations championed the cause of community and country during this national emergency. The congregation remained small, especially after the entry into Cleveland Heights of St. Martin's Chapel in 1916 and of St. Paul's Episcopal Church in 1928. In 1921, St. Alban offered to combine with St. Paul's and take its name. The offer was rejected by the larger congregation; one of the explanations was that St. Alban was too close to Lake View Cemetery. St. Alban also was denied permission by Bishop William Leonard to sell its site to interested Jewish congregations and move to the Forest Hill neighborhood. (Cleveland Public Library.)

VAN SWERINGENS' SHAKER VILLAGE, 1911. The original community of Shakers, whose barns and houses are seen in this advertisement, occupied only a small portion of the developers' subdivision that ran east and west along Fairmount Boulevard between Coventry and Ashton Roads. Nevertheless, the Van Sweringens believed the reference to the "beautiful and quaint old Shaker Settlement" would attract buyers. The Shaker community, established in 1822 by convert Ralph Russell, dissolved in 1889. (Western Reserve Historical Society.)

FAIRMOUNT BOULEVARD STREETCAR. In 1906, the Cleveland Railway Company ran its streetcar up Fairmount Boulevard through the Van Sweringens' Shaker Village. A 1907 pamphlet advertising the allotment pointed out that "the churches of Euclid and Cedar Avenues are as conveniently accessible by streetcar as from most persons' present homes." The Van Sweringens also realized that a church even closer would be better. Their later plan for the village of Shaker Heights did set aside property for a community church. (City of Cleveland Heights.)

FAIRMOUNT PRESBYTERIAN SECOND CHURCH HOME. Fairmount Presbyterian Church began as a Sunday school class that first met in the Van Sweringens' real estate office on Fairmount Boulevard in 1913. The Presbyterian Union then bought from the Van Sweringens' Shaker Heights Improvement Company a site at Coventry Road and Fairmount. Spurred by the rumors of a competing Methodist church across the boulevard (which did not materialize), the congregation built a small wooden chapel. When it was destroyed by fire two years later, the congregation built this still-modest structure. (Fairmount Presbyterian Church.)

FAIRMOUNT PRESBYTERIAN BIBLE SCHOOL, 1922. This second home of Fairmount Presbyterian Church was crowded on this spring morning. Not everyone appears to be enjoying the music. The Women's Aid Society raised $600 for the first church building and, according to the church's history, remained "a moving force within the congregation," organizing Bible study and other church activities and raising funds with church suppers and the sale of a cookbook. (Fairmount Presbyterian Church.)

FAIRMOUNT PRESBYTERIAN PALM SUNDAY, 1942. In 1921, the congregation had taken title to three more lots at Fairmount Boulevard and Scarborough Road, allowing it to begin construction of a larger building for its growing congregation. In 1924, the congregation finished a Tudor parish hall facing Scarborough. In 1939 after the worst of the Depression was over, the congregation began an even larger addition and celebrated its first worship service in this sanctuary on Palm Sunday in 1942. (Fairmount Presbyterian Church.)

CHRISTMAS EVE FAMILY SERVICE, C. 1990. Fairmount Presbyterian Church has continued the work in religious education that inspired the congregation's founding in 1913. This children's celebration of the birth of Jesus is the most beloved ritual of the Christian year. (Fairmount Presbyterian Church.)

FAIRMOUNT PRESBYTERIAN CHURCH. The tall steeple, made of wood because of a copper shortage during World War II, has remained, and the congregation has continued to add to the 1942 structure. The handsome, dignified cluster of buildings more than fulfills the 1913 prediction that this congregation would build "a great church structure." Fairmount Presbyterian Church also provided a distinguished anchor to the Van Sweringens' Shaker Village and to the neighborhood. (Fairmount Presbyterian Church.)

FAIRMOUNT BOULEVARD HOMES, 1925. Distinguished homes designed in Anglo-American styles by Meade and Hamilton in the Van Sweringens' Shaker Heights allotment set the tone for neighboring churches such as Fairmount Presbyterian Church and St. Martin's Chapel. (Western Reserve Historical Society.)

FAIRFAX SCHOOL. Like the Superior and Noble Schoolhouses, this public elementary school, completed in 1916, became the temporary home of St. Martin's Chapel and Grace Evangelical Lutheran Church. The frequent use of public space by religious congregations underscores their enthusiastic welcome by the community. (Cleveland Heights High School Alumni Foundation.)

St. Martin's Chapel. In 1917, Bishop William Leonard gave permission for the formal organization of St. Martin's congregation, which was meeting at Fairfax School. Frank A. Scott, who lived nearby on Guilford Road, donated to the congregation property at Fairmount Boulevard and Lee Roads, formerly the real estate office of the Van Sweringens' Shaker Heights Improvement Company. Architects Meade and Hamilton designed an ambitious Gothic Revival church and parish house for the congregation in keeping with their nearby Fairmount Boulevard homes. Perhaps because of wartime shortages, however, when the chapel was completed in 1919, it was a simple stucco and frame one-story building topped with a cupola. In 1927, St. Martin's Chapel was merged with St. Paul's Episcopal Church, as it planned its move to Cleveland Heights. St. Martin's property was later sold to the First Church of Christ, Scientist, Cleveland Heights. (St. Paul's Episcopal Church.)

FR. JOHN MARY POWERS. The first pastor of St. Ann Church in 1914 persuaded Bishop John P. Farrelly to loan the Meadowbrook Land Company money to buy property at Coventry and Cedar Roads on which to build both a new church and a suburban allotment, according to the church history. The loan was made secretly so that Cleveland Heights Protestants would not get wind of it. Powers hoped that Catholics settling nearby would guarantee the success of his church. Powers guided the parish until his death in 1966, playing an active role in the growing parish and suburb. (St. Ann Church.)

ST. ANN NEIGHBORHOOD, C. 1915. This first building and its garage stand alone in the woods and hay fields, although someone had already laid out formal gardens in front of these buildings. The Meadowbrook Land Company advertised that St. Ann Church would be "the only Catholic Church in Cleveland Heights. Our lots are nearest to church, school, streetcars, parks, pavements, electric lights." (St. Ann Church.)

CEDAR ROAD STREETCAR UNDER CONSTRUCTION, 1918. The streetcar referred to in the 1915 advertisement ran up Fairmount Boulevard. From there, potential homeowners had to hike to the subdivision. Fr. John Mary Powers reportedly persuaded the Cleveland Railway Company to extend this streetcar line up Cedar Road to his church's front door. (Western Reserve Historical Society.)

ST. ANN CHURCH, C. 1925. The congregation continued to grow and build, adding a handsome school, a rectory, and campanile in 1925. According to the church history, St. Ann congregants tended to be Irish Americans from the Cleveland parishes of St. Agnes, St. Thomas Aquinas, and St. Edward. More modestly priced homes allowed the Meadowbrook Land Company to compete successfully with the pricier allotments of the Van Sweringens and B. R. Deming's Euclid Golf development. (St. Ann Church.)

REMODELED ST. ANN CHURCH. After the financial difficulties of the Depression and World War II, the church underwent a dramatic renovation, completed in 1952. Its front entrance, adorned with pillars purchased by Powers in 1925 from the First National Bank, faced Coventry Road. The interior of the new sanctuary also displayed some of Powers's other purchases, including marble slabs used in the walls of the new church, bronze chandeliers, marble columns, and bronze doors. The Beaux-Arts style of the new building, designed by Walker and Weeks, differentiated St. Ann Church from the Gothic Revival Protestant churches. (St. Ann Church.)

St. Ann, Easter Sunday, 1952. This smiling crowd of formally dressed parishioners gathered outside the remodeled church to celebrate Easter Sunday and their grand, new church. This photograph shows the south entrance to the church. (St. Ann Church.)

St. Ann School Faculty, 1980–1981. St. Ann School, staffed by the Ursuline Sisters, opened in 1916 with 68 students and had 473 students in 1924, necessitating a new school building that was completed in 1925. The number of students peaked at 1,520 in 1962 and then declined steadily. In 1980, the diminishing staff of Ursulines was supplemented by lay teachers. (St. Ann Church.)

HEIGHTS UNITED PRESBYTERIAN CHURCH, C. 1922. This postcard depicts an artist's very grand version of the church at Lee Road and Washington Boulevard. The reality was a much more modest but still substantial Gothic building. The congregation disbanded in 2004, and the building is now the site of the Heights Youth Club. See page 110. (Special Collections, Cleveland State University.)

CLEVELAND HEIGHTS CITY HALL, 1924. Like the churches, Cleveland Heights government got a new home. Still located at Mayfield and Superior Roads, this brick building was designed by architect William R. Powell not in the Gothic style then associated primarily with religious structures but in a Colonial Revival style intended, like many of the suburb's street names and its domestic architecture, to evoke an Anglo-American past. (Cleveland Public Library.)

GRACE LUTHERAN CHURCH. Established in 1898 as an English-speaking congregation, Grace Lutheran Church's first house of worship was at East Fifty-fifth Street and Lexington Avenue in the Hough neighborhood. The congregation voted to move to Cleveland Heights in 1922. From 1923 until this building was finished in 1927, the pastor conducted worship services at Fairfax School and then at the Cedar Lee Theater. The brick English Gothic Revival church, designed by John C. W. Corbusier, was conveniently located on the Cedar Road streetcar line. (City of Cleveland Heights.)

GRACE LUTHERAN CHURCH SANCTUARY, C. 1936. This wedding portrait captures the soaring ceiling, elaborate wood-carved reredos, and dramatic stained-glass windows of the church. The congregation added a fellowship hall in 1967 for its expanding membership. Currently two other congregations worship at Grace Lutheran Church: the Key of Life Ministries and Holy Covenant. (Western Reserve Historical Society.)

CHURCH OF THE SAVIOUR. This elegant building dramatizes the difference between the rural community of this congregation, originally Fairmount/Heights Methodist Episcopal Church (see pages 11 and 12) and the Cleveland Heights of the 1920s. The congregation moved south to the corner of Lee and Bradford Roads, adjoining the Van Sweringens' Shaker Village allotment. Corbusier, the architect for Grace Lutheran Church, again used a multipart arched window to dramatize the front entrance. The church was dedicated in November 1928. (Church of the Saviour.)

CHURCH OF THE SAVIOUR SANCTUARY. The high vaulted ceilings, the cruciform floor plan, and the arched stained-glass windows over the altar and along the sides of the sanctuary, emphasizing height and light, are characteristic of the Gothic Revival style. The architect and congregation also planned ambitiously: the sanctuary could seat 1,100 in the nave, the two transepts, the choir stalls, and the balcony. (Church of the Saviour.)

CHURCH OF THE SAVIOUR, 1967. The congregation continued to build, adding a Sunday school wing in 1949, a bell tower in 1952, and an east wing in 1959. This aerial photograph captures the imposing presence of the church in its neighborhood. A congregation member aptly described it: "A church structure of cathedral-like proportions, a glorious monument to the Living God and an inspiration to the community and the membership." (Church of the Saviour.)

CLEVELAND HEIGHTS HIGH SCHOOL. The Cleveland Heights school board was also thinking ambitiously in the late 1920s, as evidenced by the high school completed in 1926. Its soaring columns and clock tower, like the steeples and arched windows of the new Gothic Revival churches, were intended to inspire the community. The building's size and decorative detail reflects the community's growth and prosperity. (Cleveland Heights-University Heights Board of Education.)

TRINITY CONGREGATIONAL CHURCH. Following other Cleveland churches, this congregation moved from Cedar Avenue and East Eighty-fourth Street to Cleveland Heights in 1928. The congregation built this Gothic stone structure on Washington Boulevard and sold it to Community Temple in 1947. (Western Reserve Historical Society.)

ST. PAUL'S EPISCOPAL CHURCH CONGREGATION, 1930. St. Paul's Episcopal Church left its original home on Euclid Avenue and East Fortieth Street and, like Trinity Congregational and Grace Lutheran Churches, moved to Cleveland Heights. The congregation bought the property at the intersection of Fairmount Boulevard and Coventry Road in 1924 from B. R. Deming, the developer of the Euclid Golf allotment, who judged that an Episcopalian church would be an asset to this neighborhood. The move was vigorously opposed by St. Alban Episcopal Church, which tried unsuccessfully to block it, and by Fairmount Presbyterian Church, across Coventry Road, which persuaded the Federated Churches of Cleveland to oppose the move, also unsuccessfully. St. Martin's Chapel, however, capitulated and formally merged with the larger congregation in 1928. The St. Paul's congregation is posed in front of its first building, the parish hall, used first for services on Palm Sunday in April 1928. (St. Paul's Episcopal Church.)

ST. PAUL'S SANCTUARY, C. 1936. This wedding took place in the sanctuary in the original parish hall. Rev. Walter Russell Breed, rector of St. Paul's Episcopal Church from 1907 to 1939 and the driving force behind the move to Cleveland Heights, officiated. The Depression temporarily prevented further expansion of the church. (Western Reserve Historical Society.)

ST. PAUL'S SUNDAY SCHOOL SERVICE, 1944. The congregation began work on a new sanctuary, designed by J. Byers Hayes of Walker and Weeks, in 1941, which took a decade to complete because of shortages created by World War II. Children and parents crowded into this small chapel for a wartime service. (St. Paul's Episcopal Church.)

St. Paul's Exterior, 1968. As did other mainline congregations, St. Paul's Episcopal Church flourished in the postwar period. This photograph shows the bell tower, which was completed in 1929, and the sanctuary, finally completed in 1951. When the last additions were made to St. Paul's in 1990, the church, like the Church of the Saviour, dominated the landscape and skyline of the neighborhood. (St. Paul's Episcopal Church.)

St. Paul's Youth Choir, c. 1980. Young men and women are posed in front of the elaborate carved altar screen that partially hides the Holtcamp organ, which stands at the front of the sanctuary. Under the direction of Walter Blodgett, St. Paul's Episcopal Church became known for its fine choral music. (St. Paul's Episcopal Church.)

Three

New Landscapes 1890–1959

Like Protestants and Catholics, American Jews left the cities for the suburbs roughly in the order that they arrived in this country: Germans and others from northwestern Europe before Hungarians, Russians, Poles, and Lithuanians of southeastern Europe. Like other denominations, they established congregations that reflected their varied ethnic origins as well as differences over theology and ritual, some having to do with the desired degree of assimilation into American culture. Jews, however, retained a close connection between religion and ethnicity that fostered the building of separate and distinctive institutions and neighborhoods. These often kept them relative newcomers in this country.

The first Jewish institutions in the "city of churches" moved east from the Glenville and Central neighborhoods of Cleveland and located on or near Mayfield Road. These included Mayfield Cemetery, the Oakwood Club, the Montefiore Home, the Heights Jewish Center, B'nai Jeshurun-Temple on the Heights, and Park Synagogue-Anshe Emeth Beth Tefilo. After World War II, three congregations, Beth Hamedrash Galicia-Sinai Synagogue, Shaarey Tikvah, and Beth Am-Community Temple, bought and adapted the churches of three Protestant congregations. Taylor Road became the center of Orthodox Jewish life and the location of Oheb Zedek-Taylor Road Synagogue, Congregation Shomre Shabbos, and most recently, Mosdos Ohr Hatorah school and Congregation K'hal Yereim.

Jewish congregations, like Protestant and Catholic congregations, encouraged coreligionists to move to Cleveland Heights. The growing number of Jewish institutions and homes in distinct neighborhoods along Coventry and Taylor Roads caused non-Jewish residents anxiety. Tensions surfaced, especially in the 1920s in the public schools. The architecture of Conservative and Orthodox synagogues and temples, in styles ranging from Byzantine to modern, was distinctive. Jewish shops, schools, and social service agencies also altered the suburb's physical landscape, just as their congregation members added ethnic and religious diversity to its population.

MAYFIELD CEMETERY MAUSOLEUM. The classical mausoleum is the signature building of this cemetery, established in 1890 by two Reform congregations, Tifereth Israel and Anshe Chesed. The cemetery is located just east of Lake View Cemetery on Mayfield Road. It is smaller and less grand, but like Lake View, it is a garden cemetery with impressive monuments like this mausoleum, dedicated in 1930. (James W. Garrett IV.)

MONUMENT OF RABBI BARNETT R. BRICKNER. Mayfield Cemetery is home to many leaders of Reform Judaism, including Barnett R. Brickner, the rabbi of Anshe Chesed-Euclid Avenue Temple from 1925 until his death in 1958. The congregation moved to Beachwood in 1957, becoming Fairmount Temple. Brickner gave the graduation address at Cleveland Heights High School in 1932, his presence acknowledging the importance of the suburb's Jewish community. (Author's collection.)

OAKWOOD CLUB. Established in 1905 at Mayfield and Warrensville Center Roads by Cleveland's Jewish elite, this golf club was the Jewish alternative to Patrick Calhoun's Euclid Club. Its 18-hole golf course was completed in 1915 and became the site of national golf tournaments. Oakwood merged in 1931 with the Excelsior Club. (Case Western Reserve University Special Collections.)

MONTEFIORE HOME. Originally for elderly, needy Jews, the residence moved from its location at East Fifty-fifth Street and Woodland Avenue in Cleveland to property on Mayfield Road purchased from O. A. Dean in 1919. This photograph was taken about 1941. Architect Charles Greco designed this building in a traditional Georgian Revival style, anticipating the style of Cleveland Heights City Hall that would soon be built just to the west. The Montefiore Home moved to Beachwood in 1996. (Western Reserve Historical Society.)

HEIGHTS JEWISH CENTER. This congregation organized in Cleveland Heights in 1923 as the Heights Jewish Orthodox Congregation and worshipped first in a home on Euclid Heights Boulevard and then in the Heights Theater at Euclid Heights Boulevard and Coventry Road. In 1928, the congregation purchased this large home on Superior Road, which became the Heights Jewish Center. In 1947, the congregation built the brick building behind the home. In 1979, the congregation moved to University Heights. (City of Cleveland Heights.)

B'NAI JESHURUN-TEMPLE ON THE HEIGHTS GROUNDBREAKING, 1924. This congregation had earlier purchased a property at Derbyshire Road and Euclid Heights Boulevard, later rejected either because it was too small or because the zoning did not permit the building. After this 1924 groundbreaking, construction at this site on Mayfield Road was halted for two months while the congregation considered swapping it for a much larger 16-acre parcel on Superior Road offered by John D. Rockefeller Jr. Construction was resumed after the deal fell through. (Western Reserve Historical Society.)

B'NAI JESHURUN-TEMPLE ON THE HEIGHTS. This became the first Jewish house of worship built in Cleveland Heights. The Conservative congregation was renamed Temple on the Heights. Rabbi Abraham Nowak led the congregation. Charles Greco designed this Byzantine-inspired building with two-and-a-half-story pillars at the entrance and a 12-sided central dome that provided a striking contrast with the steeples and turrets of nearby churches. The temple's official opening in 1926 was attended by many dignitaries, including Fr. John Mary Powers and Mayor Frank Cain. Intended to serve all the needs of the rapidly growing Jewish community, the sprawling, impressive facility also included a library, bowling alleys, a dining room, and a ballroom. The wing to the right was added in 1956. (Western Reserve Historical Society.)

B'NAI JESHURUN SANCTUARY. When the building was completed, this sanctuary was intended to seat 2,000, and another auditorium seated 1,200. The rather austere interior contrasts with the elaborate ornamentation of the building's facade. (Western Reserve Historical Society.)

B'NAI JESHURUN FLAG RAISING, 1941. Like other Cleveland Heights residents, Jews enthusiastically supported United States' participation in World War II. This ceremony and the United States flag displayed in the sanctuary express that support as well as the congregation's continuing efforts to assimilate into the community. In 1980, the congregation moved to Pepper Pike. (Western Reserve Historical Society.)

BOULEVARD SCHOOL. In 1924, Protestant congregations initiated a short-lived effort to have students released from public school an hour a week for religious education in nearby churches. Children from Boulevard School, for example, would go to Messiah Lutheran Church. Bishop Joseph Schrembs and several rabbis successfully protested that the arrangement violated the separation of church and state. In 1937, an estimated 31.3 percent of Cleveland Heights' public school population was Jewish. Eventually Yom Kippur became a public school holiday in Cleveland Heights. (Cleveland Heights-University Heights Board of Education.)

COVENTRY ROAD, C. 1928. Close to B'nai Jeshurun, the Heights Jewish Center, and the Montefiore Home, Coventry Road became a bustling Jewish commercial center by the late 1920s. The 1929 city directory listed many Jewish merchants, including Charles Benjamin, tailor; Hyman Debowitz, baker; Robert Katz, meats; Joseph Wasserman, fruits; Rothkopf Brothers, dairy; Bruder Brothers, butter and eggs; as well as a Kroger's and a Piggly Wiggly grocery. (Western Reserve Historical Society.)

Park School. In 1929, the progressive day school moved to this site on Euclid Heights Boulevard that belonged to John D. Rockefeller Jr., who deeded it to the school three years later. The school's teaching philosophy meshed with the informality of the small, loosely connected wooden buildings, and the school encouraged its students to take advantage of the woods, streams, and ravines of this natural setting. The school closed in 1942, and the property was sold to Anshe Emeth congregation. (Western Reserve Historical Society.)

Park Day Camp. At the time it purchased this property, Anshe Emeth congregation was located on East 105th Street in Glenville, where it had built an enormous complex known as the Cleveland Jewish Center. As its congregation moved east, however, Anshe Emeth supported two small extension programs in Cleveland Heights. Even before building its house of worship, it opened a school and this day camp in 1943. (Western Reserve Historical Society.)

PARK SYNAGOGUE-ANSHE EMETH BETH TEFILO CONGREGATION. The congregation, led by Rabbi Armond Cohen, chose internationally known architect Eric Mendelsohn to design this modern structure. Unlike the Byzantine-inspired Temple on the Heights, this synagogue's unadorned curves make no historic references. In 1947, as Mendelsohn's plans took shape, neighbors, especially those on adjoining Compton Road, vigorously opposed the new building: Jewish institutions already outnumbered those of any other denomination, they maintained. The opponents lost this battle, however, and Cleveland Heights gained perhaps the most dramatic modern structure in the Greater Cleveland area. (Vivian Gladden.)

PARK SYNAGOGUE THANKSGIVING INTERFAITH SERVICE, 1951. After Park Synagogue was dedicated in 1950, the congregation hosted this interfaith service, part of its ongoing effort to make peace with the neighbors and the community. The spacious sanctuary was designed to seat 1,000. (Western Reserve Historical Society.)

PARK SYNAGOGUE INTERIOR, 2006. The circle is the dominant theme of the building. The shape of the dome is echoed by the circular sanctuary. Its clear windows flood the space with light and connect worshipers to the beauty of the natural setting. The seating under the central dome fans out from the ark on a mahogany bimah. (Park Synagogue.)

CONGREGATION BETH AM-COMMUNITY TEMPLE. This congregation, a splinter group of B'nai Jeshurun led by Rabbi Abraham Nowak, purchased Trinity Congregational Church in 1947, building an addition but otherwise keeping the Gothic exterior. In 1999, it rejoined B'nai Jeshurun and moved to Pepper Pike. (City of Cleveland Heights.)

HEBREW ACADEMY, 1953. This was the second Orthodox institution in Cleveland Heights when it opened in 1949 and the first of many on Taylor Road. The school provided a full secular and religious education to students from kindergarten to high school, helping to maintain Jewish identity in this suburban setting. The building is also the home of a branch of the Young Israel congregation. (Western Reserve Historical Society.)

OHEB ZEDEK-TAYLOR ROAD SYNAGOGUE. This Orthodox congregation, dating back to 1904, was joined by several smaller Orthodox congregations when it moved to Cleveland Heights. This building, designed in the international style by Milo Holdstein, took two years to complete; it was dedicated in 1951. The synagogue's curving lines differentiate it from both the Gothic Revival churches of the 1920s and the Colonial Revival churches of the post–World War II period. (City of Cleveland Heights.)

OHEB ZEDEK-TAYLOR ROAD SYNAGOGUE SANCTUARY. Stained-glass windows incorporating Jewish symbols encircle the sanctuary, making distinctive both the interior and the exterior of the synagogue. (Oheb Zedek-Taylor Road Synagogue.)

SHAAREY TIKVAH. This congregation of German origin purchased the home of the Cleveland Heights Presbyterian Church at Mayfield and Preyer Roads in 1950, keeping the exterior intact while altering the interior for its own services. The Presbyterians moved across the street into the Forest Hill neighborhood and became Forest Hill Church. The Jewish congregation is now located in Beachwood. (Western Reserve Historical Society.)

BETH HAMEDRASH GALICIA-SINAI SYNAGOGUE. The congregation came to Cleveland Heights from Glenville and bought this building at Desota and Berkeley Avenues from Messiah Lutheran Church. The Jewish congregation dedicated the building in 1953. To the original Gothic structure, the congregation added the Colonial entrance to the left, in keeping with the current architectural styles for suburban churches. (City of Cleveland Heights.)

CONGREGATION SHOMRE SHABBOS. In 1956, this Orthodox congregation with Hungarian origins broke ground on Taylor Road for a distinctive, modern brick-and-stone building designed by architect Arthur M. Hemlock. Steps lead from the sidewalk to the building whose curving lines are reminiscent of Oheb Zedek and Park Synagogue. (Author's collection.)

CONGREGATION ZEMACH ZEDEK. This small building on Lee Road housed a drugstore in the 1920s. In 1958, this Orthodox congregation joined Heights Ahaveth Sholem congregation at this location. Zemach Zedek now serves some of the recent émigrés from the former Soviet Union, who make up the newest Jewish population in Cleveland Heights. (Author's collection.)

MARMAROSHER SHUL. The congregation, also from Glenville, moved into this new building on Lancashire Road in 1952. It was the last Jewish institution to be built in the Coventry Road neighborhood; Taylor Road replaced Coventry as the center of Jewish life. In 1975, the congregation sold the building to the Unitarian Universalist Society and moved to Beachwood. (City of Cleveland Heights.)

CONGREGATION KEHILLAT YAAKOV-WARRENSVILLE CENTER SYNAGOGUE. This congregation, created by the merger of eight small Orthodox congregations with origins in several ethnic groups, moved into this contemporary building designed by Sigmund Braverman in 1959. The facility, just east of the Oakwood Club, is now owned by Mosdos Ohr Hotorah, and the congregation built a new synagogue in Lyndhurst. (City of Cleveland Heights.).

Congregation K'hal Yereim. This small building originally housed an office. This congregation purchased the building from another Orthodox congregation, Heichal Habrocho, and redesigned the exterior using Jerusalem stone. The contemporary style contrasts with Taylor Road's shops built in the 1920s and the homes of the neighborhood, mostly brick Colonials built in the 1940s. (James W. Garrett IV.)

Mosdos Ohr Hotorah. The newest Jewish institution in Cleveland Heights is this school on Taylor Road, built in 1997. It is also the house of worship of the Ahas Yisroel congregation. This contemporary building emphasizes contrasting shapes, colors, and textures. It houses the girls' department of the school; the boys' department is located in the Warrensville Center Synagogue building. (James W. Garrett IV.)

Four

TRANSFORMATIONS 1926–1963

The movement of religious congregations from the city into the suburbs continued during these decades, slowing briefly during the Depression, accelerating again in the postwar period, and bringing with it not only new houses of worship but also new denominational institutions. This movement coincided with the decline of the great mansions that defined the elite status of older suburbs.

These circumstances created opportunities for Protestant, Catholic, and Jewish institutions to move into Cleveland Heights, transforming some of the suburb's earliest and grandest homes. These changes began in the late 1920s in Patrick Calhoun's Euclid Heights allotment. Newer, less-formal homes in allotments like the Van Sweringens' Shaker Village and B. R. Deming's Euclid Golf made these mansions, built from the 1890s through the second decade of the 20th century, less fashionable. The property taxes of the Depression and wartime shortages of building materials and servants made it difficult, even for the wealthy, to maintain their enormous homes.

Into these estates and formerly exclusive neighborhoods moved four Catholic institutions, Ursuline College, the Carmelite Monastery, Beaumont School, and the Catharine Horstmann Home; two Lutheran institutions, First English Lutheran Church and Lutheran East High School; the Baptist Home of Northern Ohio and Cedar Hill Baptist Church; the First Church of Christ, Scientist, Cleveland, and across the street, Overlook House, a Christian Science retirement facility; and the Jewish Community Center and the Jewish-sponsored Council Gardens housing complex. A Jewish congregation and a Jewish rabbinical school did not succeed in moving in.

By 1960, these transformations seemed to signal an end to the era when the socially elite families of bankers, industrialists, and professionals chose Cleveland Heights as their home. Consequently, although these changes created controversy, religious institutions helped to ease the painful transition by maintaining and adapting the original buildings or by preventing the incursion of commerce into residential neighborhoods.

OVERLOOK ROAD. Seen from across the Euclid Heights Boulevard–Cedar Road intersection, this street of grand homes was intended to be the crown jewel of Patrick Calhoun's Euclid Heights allotment, the suburban version of Cleveland's "millionaires' row," Euclid Avenue. Calhoun succeeded in attracting some of Cleveland's elite to this site, high on a bluff overlooking the city and the lake. On the left are the homes of lawyer Hermon O. Kelley, industrialist Loftus Cuddy, lawyer Samuel Dodge, and banker William Sherwin. To the right is the mansion of Howard P. Eells. Overlook Road constituted the western boundary of the allotment and runs across the boundary between Cleveland and Cleveland Heights. The streetcar that Calhoun built to serve the residents of his development also attracted the institutions that moved on to Overlook Road. (Nottingham Spirk and Design.)

URSULINE COLLEGE, 1930. When Hermon O. Kelley died in 1925, this home was advertised for sale not as a Tudor mansion in an exclusive residential neighborhood but as "an ideal apartment or family hotel site." Its buyer in 1927 was not a wealthy Cleveland family but Ursuline College. The college used the Kelley home as a library and bought the Cuddy home next door for a classroom and administration building. (Ursuline College.)

URSULINE COLLEGE DORMITORY. In 1944, the college purchased the handsome Georgian Revival John Sherwin mansion. After Ursuline College moved to Pepper Pike in 1959, it briefly retained this house as a dormitory. Through the 1960s, Case Institute of Technology (now Case Western Reserve University) purchased the Ursuline College properties, razed them, and built tennis courts and a small park on their sites. (Ursuline College.)

HOWELL HINDS HOME. This formidable Romanesque mansion north of the Ursuline buildings and also in Cleveland was completed in 1899. Its landscaped gardens sloped down the hill behind the mansion. The 1900 census described Howell Hinds simply as a "capitalist" and listed the Hinds' six live-in servants. Hinds also built a carriage house across Overlook Road on what is now Herrick Mews. (Nottingham Spirk and Design.)

FIRST CHURCH OF CHRIST, SCIENTIST, CLEVELAND UNDER CONSTRUCTION. After Hinds's death in 1926, his widow sold the property to this congregation, which demolished the mansion and began construction of this imposing neoclassical house of worship. The congregation was organized in 1888 and moved to Cleveland Heights from its church at Euclid Avenue and East Ninety-third Street, the former home of the Euclid Avenue Methodist Church. (Nottingham Spirk and Design.)

First Church of Christ, Scientist, Cleveland. Designed by the firm of Walker and Weeks and completed in 1930, this is considered to be one of the firm's most distinguished buildings and the model for their design of Severance Hall, the home of the Cleveland Orchestra. The entrance portico is supported by classical pillars, and the auditorium behind is octagonal in shape, a form often used in Christian Science churches. The freestanding tower, illuminated at night, made this congregation a visible presence for miles. (Nottingham Spirk and Design.)

ROLLIN H. WHITE HOME. Rollin H. White was the founder of White Motor Company, a manufacturer of automobiles. This artist's rendition of his home at Fairmount Boulevard and Lee Road appeared in a 1904 advertisement for the Van Sweringens' Shaker Heights allotment. The opportunity to have the industrialist as a neighbor was intended to attract other wealthy buyers. (Shaker Historical Society.)

CARMELITE MONASTERY. In 1935, the Cleveland Carmel of the Holy Family, a contemplative order, bought the White property, moved from St. Clair Avenue, and used the White home as its monastery until 1962 when this new building was completed. This was the first religious institution at this intersection. Beaumont School; the First Church of Christ, Scientist, Cleveland Heights; and the Jewish True Sisters Child Care Center followed. (Catholic Universe Bulletin.)

First English Lutheran Church. The property at Euclid Heights and Derbyshire Road, purchased in 1923 for B'nai Jeshurun, was sold to this Lutheran congregation in 1932 for $20,000, probably a Depression bargain. The congregation moved to Cleveland Heights from East 105th Street and Chester Avenue but quickly ran into financial difficulties when the Guardian Trust bank failed, impounding the church's building funds. The church remained half-built until 1936. (First English Lutheran Church.)

Warren Bicknell Mansion. In 1939, this impressive home of industrialist and philanthropist Warren Bicknell in the Ambler Heights allotment was sold to the Baptist Home of Northern Ohio. The home is now Judson Park, part of the Judson Retirement Center, and the only institution in this neighborhood, now called Chestnut Hills. (Special Collections, Cleveland State University.)

KENYON V. PAINTER ESTATE. Banker Kenyon V. Painter built this Tudor mansion in 1904 on 28 acres at the corner of Fairmount Boulevard and Lee Roads just east of the Rollin H. White home in the Van Sweringens' Shaker Heights allotment. Painter also maintained a private zoo and deer park on the property with a wall along Fairmount Boulevard to enclose the animals. (Western Reserve Historical Society.)

BEAUMONT SCHOOL DEDICATION, 1942. After Painter's death, the estate was sold to the Ursuline Sisters for this girls' school, which became the second Ursuline institution in Cleveland Heights. The new facility was named for Mother Mary of the Annunciation Beaumont, the first Ursuline Mother Superior in Cleveland. This dedication service was attended by hundreds of Ursuline nuns from Cleveland and northeast Ohio. (Catholic Universe Bulletin.)

HOWARD P. EELLS MANSION. Frank Meade designed this English-style home for banker and philanthropist Howard P. Eells. The home occupied a prominent site at the corner of Overlook Road and Euclid Heights Boulevard at the top of Cedar Glen. The Community Temple's efforts to lease the property were rebuffed by the city in 1943. An apartment house was built at this location after the site was rezoned. (Western Reserve Historical Society.)

CATHERINE HORSTMANN HOME. This Catholic agency, originally a home for working girls, purchased the John R. Chandler home on Overlook Road in 1951 and left the house intact. Across the street from Ursuline College, this became the second Catholic institution on Overlook Road. (Cleveland Catholic Diocesan Archives.)

MYRON HERRICK HOME ON OVERLOOK. A former Cleveland city councilman (1885–1890), governor of Ohio (1903–1905), and U.S. ambassador to France under the presidencies of William Howard Taft and Warren G. Harding, Myron Herrick is said to have entertained his close friend Pres. William McKinley in this home. Although on the east side of Overlook Road, the handsome home was within the Cleveland city limits. Herrick sold the home to industrialist Benedict Crowell. (Western Reserve Historical Society.)

OVERLOOK HOUSE. Crowell in turn sold the home in 1949 to Northern Ohio Trustees Inc. This corporation used the Herrick mansion for Overlook House, a Christian Science retirement center, until the mansion was replaced in the 1970s by this contemporary building directly across the street from the First Church of Christ, Scientist, Cleveland. (Author's collection.)

Patrick Calhoun Mansion on Cedar Road. Patrick Calhoun began construction of this enormous home in 1903. It reportedly had 30 bedrooms (a local newspaper called it a "Florentine pile"). Calhoun ran into financial and political difficulties in San Francisco, and the home was not completed until 1911. By then, his Euclid Heights allotment was also on the skids, and when his creditors closed in, Calhoun barely retained control of the mansion, claiming that it belonged to his wife. When he went bankrupt in 1914, his home and its four-and-a-half-acre site were sold to Dr. George W. Crile, a surgeon and a founder of the Cleveland Clinic. After Crile's death, the Telshe Rabbinical College in 1943 asked permission to buy the home, promising to leave it intact. The Cleveland Heights Planning and Zoning Commission denied permission, as the neighbors objected strenuously. (Cleveland Public Library.)

CEDAR HILL BAPTIST CHURCH. Neighbors and city officials did permit the construction of Cedar Hill Baptist Church on the site of the Calhoun/Crile mansion. Architects Dalton and Dalton Associates designed the simple but gracious brick building. The congregation, then named Hough Avenue Baptist Church, had lost its house of worship at Hough Avenue and East Eighty-second Street to a fire in 1953. In 1955, after purchasing the property, the congregation changed its name and, in 1956, moved to Cleveland Heights. (Cedar Hill Baptist Church.)

CEDAR HILL BAPTIST SANCTUARY. The simple interior echoes the building's exterior. The congregation's sprawling one-story complex, which includes Cedar Hill Christian School, complements rather than dominates the neighborhood. (Author's collection.)

GLEN ALLEN ESTATE, 1928. The large estate on Mayfield Road east of Taylor Road was originally the Severance family's summer home. In 1915, Elizabeth Severance Allen, recently widowed, commissioned Charles Schweinfurth, the architect for many Euclid Avenue homes, to design this imposing mansion. She named the estate Glen Allen after her late husband, Dr. Dudley P. Allen. She married Francis Fleury Prentiss in 1917. The often-photographed estate was famous for its formal gardens. After her death in 1945, the home was demolished, and the property to the north was developed as single-family homes. (Western Reserve Historical Society.)

LUTHERAN EAST HIGH SCHOOL. Part of the Mayfield Road frontage of Glen Allen became the site of Lutheran East High School, one of three new Lutheran institutions in Cleveland Heights. This location was originally considered as the possible site for a second public high school until voters in 1957 turned down the bond issue to pay for the new building. This school opened in 1960. It is also the worship site for Newsong Church, a member of the Assemblies of God denomination. (Author's collection.)

JEWISH COMMUNITY CENTER. To the west of Lutheran East High School, the remaining frontage of Glen Allen became the Jewish Community Center after a vigorous battle that pitted unsuccessful neighbors against Cleveland Heights City Council. Completed in 1960, the center housed a wide variety of cultural and recreational programs until it was sold to a developer in 2004. The contemporary sculpture honored David Berger, a Cleveland athlete competing for Israel when he was murdered during the 1972 Olympic games. (City of Cleveland Heights.)

BEN BRAE ESTATE. Elisabeth Severance Allen Prentiss's cousin Julia and her husband, Dr. Benjamin Millikin, built this gracious Tudor Revival home in 1913 just to the west of Glen Allen. Ben Brae was demolished in 1953. (Western Reserve Historical Society.)

BEN BRAE GARDENS. Although it was less formal than Glen Allen, Ben Brae was also noted for the extensive formal gardens behind the home. On the horizon, Lake Erie was visible on a clear day. (Western Reserve Historical Society.)

COUNCIL GARDENS. On the site of the former Ben Brae gardens, the National Council of Jewish Women sponsored this contemporary one-story retirement facility that opened in 1963. The sloping woods and lawns retain the feel of the Ben Brae gardens. The City of Cleveland Heights built a fire station on the portion of the Millikin property that fronted on Mayfield Road. (Author's collection.)

Five

COLONIAL REVIVALS 1939–1960

World War II renewed American prosperity and Americans' interest in organized religion. Both spurred the movement of new religious congregations into the suburbs and the building of new homes in the suburbs for old congregations.

In 1960, Cleveland Heights' population hit an all-time high, as did the number of its religious congregations. The Cleveland Heights city manager listed 44 houses of worship in the suburb; four Jewish congregations held services in public schools. New congregations included First Church of Christ, Scientist, Cleveland Heights; St. Louis Church (Roman Catholic); Bethel Baptist Church (Bethel Church of Cleveland Heights); Bethlehem Lutheran Church; Church of the Blessed Hope (Church of God); Hope Lutheran Church; Euclid Avenue Christian Church (Disciples of Christ); the Church of Christ at Forest Hill; the Church of the Master (American Baptist); and SS. Constantine and Helen Greek Orthodox Cathedral. Older congregations, including Forest Hill Presbyterian Church (formerly Cleveland Heights Presbyterian), Noble Road Presbyterian Church, and Church of the Redeemer United Methodist, built new churches. Congregations sparked a new building boom.

Religious pluralism accentuated the suburb's growing ethnic and class diversity. Despite these differences, or perhaps because of them, many new and old churches chose to build in a nostalgic American Colonial Revival style. Its simple, classical columns and pediment topped with a steeple evoked a distant New England past. The style was compatible with Cleveland Heights' homes and public buildings built from about 1900 to 1930 and especially with newer postwar homes and public structures. Unlike the Gothic churches of the 1920s, these were intended to accommodate not dominate the surrounding landscape. Compared to the earlier ambitious architect-designed churches, these were simple and relatively inexpensive to build. At least four congregations helped to build their own churches.

FIRST CHURCH OF CHRIST, SCIENTIST, CLEVELAND HEIGHTS, 1939. This classic Colonial Revival church with white pillars that frame the entrance and a steeple that announces a Christian presence set the precedent for many Cleveland Heights churches of the post–World War II period. Its site at the intersection of Fairmount Boulevard and Lee Road was the former home of St. Martin's Chapel. (First Church of Christ, Scientist, Cleveland.)

FIRST CHURCH OF CHRIST, SCIENTIST, INTERIOR, 2008. The interior is as simple as the exterior. Words from the New Testament appear to the left of the lectern. The words of Mary Baker Eddy, founder of the denomination, are on the right. This congregation merged with First Church of Christ, Scientist, Cleveland in 2004. (Cyndy Bernheimer.)

ST. LOUIS CHURCH'S SECOND HOME. The Roman Catholic congregation celebrated its first mass on Christmas Eve in 1947 in the Center-Mayfield movie theater. This unpretentious basement of the church's rectory on Edendale and Mayfield Roads served as a second home for the congregation. (St. Louis Church.)

ST. LOUIS CHURCH AND SCHOOL. The congregation originally wanted to purchase a site in the Rockefellers' Forest Hill allotment but was denied permission to build a school. Instead, it purchased the northernmost portion of Elizabeth Severance Allen's estate north of Council Gardens. The church and school were dedicated in 1951. (Cleveland Catholic Diocesan Archives.)

ST. LOUIS SCHOOL FOURTH- AND FIFTH-GRADE GIRLS' SOFTBALL. St. Louis School's first students attended St. Gregory School from 1949 until 1951, when their own school building opened. The Felician Sisters of St. Francis staffed the school. Grades one through eight enrolled 344 students. The student body peaked at 583 but declined after 1965. The school closed in 2007. (St. Louis Church.)

ST. LOUIS CHURCH SANCTUARY. In the wake of the Second Vatican Council, the congregation remodeled the sanctuary, dedicated in 1973. Above the altar hangs a stylized bronze crucifix designed by sculptor William McVey. Stained-glass windows were installed in 1978. In honor of its golden jubilee, the congregation remodeled the sanctuary again. As Catholic churches across the diocese and the country close, St. Louis will merge with St. Ann Church. (St. Louis Church.)

FOREST HILL PRESBYTERIAN CHURCH. In 1945, this congregation, formerly Cleveland Heights Presbyterian Church, purchased property in the Rockefellers' Forest Hill allotment that the developers, like the Van Sweringens, set aside for a community church. The congregation moved from its location at Mayfield and Preyer Roads, sold the building to Shaarey-Tikvah congregation, and dedicated this handsome Colonial building in 1951 at the prominent intersection of Monticello and Lee Boulevards. Its tall steeple is the church's most dramatic feature. The new homes nearby were designed in compatible styles. (Forest Hill Presbyterian Church.)

FOREST HILL SANCTUARY, MAY 1964. The growing congregation soon required the church to expand. Adult and youth choirs performed for this overflow crowd in the new sanctuary. On this formal occasion, the women wore hats and furs; the men were in suits and ties. (Forest Hill Presbyterian Church.)

FOREST HILL SANCTUARY, 2007. Like that of other major Protestant denominations, the membership of Forest Hill Church has declined since its peak years of the 1960s. This photograph looks from the altar to the back of the church, capturing a smaller, less formal but no less worshipful congregation. (Forest Hill Presbyterian Church.)

CHURCH OF THE REDEEMER UNITED METHODIST. When this church, originally Cleveland Heights Evangelical Mission, was remodeled in the 1980s, the 1924 wooden building was removed (see page 24). The Colonial character of the 1950 building at Taylor and Scarborough Roads was reemphasized. The gracious, informal brick church lends dignity to this residential neighborhood. (Kathryn Klaber.)

CHURCH OF THE REDEEMER, EASTER SUNDAY, 1952. Like the Forest Hill Presbyterians, these Methodists are formally dressed for an Easter service. The flowering lilies celebrate the resurrection of Christ. (Church of the Redeemer United Methodist.)

CHURCH OF THE REDEEMER CONGREGATION, 2007. More than a half century later, both the sanctuary and the congregation had a new look. Gathered on the altar rather than in the pews, these members, old and young, black and white, joyfully face the camera. (Carolyn Shepherd and Marj Craft.)

NOBLE ROAD PRESBYTERIAN CHURCH. In 1924, the congregation added a substantial extension to the 1909 building (see page 21), and as the congregation and the neighborhood expanded in the postwar years, it remodeled the front of the old church in the Colonial style. The building was rededicated in 1951. The substantial columns, solemn doors, and ascending steps announce the church's new entrance. The elaborate cupola and spire point heavenward but also accentuate the church's presence in the here and now. (City of Cleveland Heights.)

Noble Road Presbyterian Church Worship Service. The cheerful informality of the worship services of some Protestant churches is illustrated here by the musician-pastor and his youthful accompanists. (Noble Road Presbyterian Church.)

Noble Road Presbyterians on Parade, 1996. Like other congregations, Noble Road Presbyterian Church participated in the parade that celebrated Cleveland Heights' 75 years as a city. Adults and children carried this colorful banner. (Author's collection.)

HOPE LUTHERAN CHURCH. This congregation, whose roots go back to the German-speaking Peace Lutheran Church, moved to Cleveland Heights from the Glenville neighborhood. The congregation purchased this site at Northvale and Taylor Roads at the northeast end of the growing Forest Hill development. Stone surrounds the front door, also accented by the stone crucifix and stained-glass windows. More Gothic than Colonial, the building was dedicated in 1952. In 1964, the congregation added an education wing, used today for preschool and music programs. (Hope Lutheran Church.)

HOPE LUTHERAN SANCTUARY. As the community changed and its membership began to decline in the 1980s and 1990s, the church adapted as well. Hope Lutheran Church became a racially integrated congregation and, in 2001, a Reconciling in Christ congregation. (Hope Lutheran Church.)

HOPE LUTHERAN MEMBERS AT THE SCHWAN CHRISTMAS TREE. The congregation remembers its German roots by decorating this Christmas tree, planted at Lake View Cemetery to honor Rev. Henry C. Schwan, who was reportedly the first American pastor to introduce a Christmas tree into a church sanctuary. (Hope Lutheran Church.)

Bethlehem Lutheran Church. This congregation was founded in 1889 as the Swedish Evangelical Lutheran Bethlehem Church of Cleveland. The congregation bought its property at Mayfield and Crest Roads in 1945. When it moved to Cleveland Heights, the congregation, like St. Louis Church, worshipped in the Center Mayfield Theater in 1953 until the building was completed in 1954 with the help of members of the congregation. Like Hope Lutheran Church, this structure is more Gothic than Colonial. (City of Cleveland Heights.)

Church of the Blessed Hope. This congregation was originally organized in 1863 as a Church of God. When it moved to Cleveland Heights in 1953, its name was changed to the Church of the Blessed Hope. In 1976, the congregation sold this small Colonial-style building at Fairmount Boulevard and Taylor Road to the Greater Peace Missionary Baptist Church and moved to Chesterland. (City of Cleveland Heights.)

Bethel Church of Cleveland Heights. When this church, first organized in 1889 as the First Swedish Baptist Church of Cleveland, moved to Cleveland Heights from Cleveland, it worshipped at Noble School. In the spring of 1952, the congregation's first services were held in a chapel at its present location on Noble Road, purchased from Heights Assembly of God (Pentecostal). (James W. Garrett IV.)

Bethel Church of Cleveland Heights Sanctuary. In 1955, the congregation laid the cornerstone for the large contemporary building that included this simple, light-filled sanctuary. Men of the congregation did much of the work on the new building, which was dedicated in 1957. (Bethel Church of Cleveland Heights.)

THE CHURCH OF THE MASTER. The result of the merger of several congregations, this American Baptist congregation became the Church of the Master in 1921. Pressure from friends and members of the congregation persuaded the City of Cleveland Heights to sell this property at Monticello Boulevard and Quarry Road to the church. Denison Park was completed in 1955 on the rest of the city property. (Special Collections, Cleveland State University.)

THE CHURCH OF THE MASTER SANCTUARY. The congregation worshipped at Oxford School from 1952 until the building, designed by Copper, Wade, and Associates, was dedicated in 1953. Congregation members helped put the finishing touches on the building's interior. (Church of the Master.)

EUCLID AVENUE CHRISTIAN CHURCH. Architect George Kramer designed this Romanesque building with its rough, green stone exterior, multiple gables, and elegant stained-glass windows for this Disciples of Christ congregation, which was founded in 1843. This building was completed in 1908 on Euclid Avenue. In 1955, the congregation moved to Cleveland Heights. For half a century after its move, the congregation was known as Euclid Avenue Christian Church and only recently was rechristened Disciples Christian Church. The congregation sold this building on Euclid Avenue to East Mount Zion Baptist Church. (Special Collections, Cleveland State University.)

DISCIPLES CHRISTIAN CHURCH. The contrast between the elaborate Euclid Avenue church and the congregation's traditional Colonial Revival church in Cleveland Heights illustrates changing styles in ecclesiastical architecture. The church at Mayfield and Yellowstone Roads was completed in 1955. Multiple pillars mark the entrance to the one-story brick building. A ceramic sculpture, *Christ and the Children*, by Thelma Frazier Winter, hangs on the south outside wall. Only the simple steeple calls attention to the church. This is also the home of the Heights Emergency Food Center. (Disciples Christian Church.)

DISCIPLES CHRISTIAN CHURCH JOURNEY TO BETHLEHEM. This annual event for the community celebrated the birth of Christ with real animals and a crowd of worshippers, including this rather apprehensive shepherd. According to the church's history, the pageant "focuses our attention back to the true meaning of Christmas—the little town, the Christ Child and the story that continues to inspire humankind after 2,000 years." (Disciples Christian Church.)

DISCIPLES CHRISTIAN CHURCH WORSHIP SERVICE. The children's choir also celebrated the Christmas season. When Cleveland Heights' population began to change, its religious congregations welcomed African Americans into the community. (Disciples Christian Church.)

SS. Constantine and Helen Greek Orthodox Cathedral. Steps lead up from Mayfield Road to this dramatic Byzantine-inspired entrance of the cathedral, designed by Carr and Cunningham. Like Christian churches and Jewish synagogues and temples, the architecture of this house of worship is intended to evoke the history and culture of the ethnic groups that built it. (City of Cleveland Heights.)

SS. Constantine and Helen Opening of the Doors, September 1957. The congregation acquired the property in 1953, broke ground in 1956, and held this solemn ceremony attended by visiting Greek Orthodox clergy in 1957. The congregation's first regular service was Christmas Eve in 1957. (SS. Constantine and Helen Greek Orthodox Cathedral.)

MAKING *LOUKOMADES* AT SS. CONSTANTINE AND HELEN, 1978. Religious congregations help to sustain the ethnic identity of their members in a variety of ways, including use of the original language in worship services, the iconography, and the food of the country of origin. (Special Collections, Cleveland State University.)

SS. CONSTANTINE AND HELEN GREEK FESTIVAL. This annual event attracts visitors from all over the Cleveland area every August. It celebrates Greek culture, raises funds for the cathedral, and reminds Cleveland Heights to celebrate its ethnic diversity. (SS. Constantine and Helen Greek Orthodox Cathedral.)

CHURCH OF CHRIST AT FOREST HILL CONGREGATION, 1959. The congregation, then located at Shaw Avenue in East Cleveland, purchased this three-acre lot at Mayfield and Taylor Roads in 1957. These hopeful members gathered at the site of their future home on the edge of the Forest Hill allotment shortly after the groundbreaking ceremonies in 1959. (Church of Christ at Forest Hill.)

CHURCH OF CHRIST AT FOREST HILL CONGREGATION AT WORK. Like other congregations in this era, the Church of Christ put its members and pastor to work, raising the roof as well as finishing the interior of the building. The congregation hired a construction firm to do the general contracting, but volunteers' hours saved the congregation thousands of dollars. (Church of Christ at Forest Hill.)

CHURCH OF CHRIST AT FOREST HILL. The modest brick building was completed in 1960. Its only decorative element is the brickwork marking the building's entrance. The church's spire marks the top of the rise of Mayfield. This congregation joined Bethlehem Lutheran Church, Lutheran East High School, Euclid Avenue/Disciples Christian Church, and SS. Constantine and Helen Greek Orthodox Cathedral near this busy intersection. (Church of Christ at Forest Hill.)

Church of Christ Interior, 2008. The simple auditorium is windowless; the stained-glass window is its focal point. The roofline of the building, assembled by volunteers almost half a century earlier, is still visible. (Church of Christ at Forest Hill.)

Church of Christ Kids Day Jubilee Olympics, 1996. This annual event celebrates the achievements of the congregation's children. They carry flags to honor themselves. Like other Cleveland Heights congregations, this one has become a church home to its African American neighbors. (Church of Christ at Forest Hill.)

COVENTRY SCHOOL. Completed in 1919, this elementary school in 1962 also served as the temporary home of Lancashire Religious School. The building was demolished in 1976 and replaced by a smaller building, which was closed in 2007. (Cleveland Heights High School Alumni Foundation.)

TAYLOR SCHOOL. In 1962, the United Jewish Religious Group worshiped in this elementary school in the Jewish neighborhood. Perhaps the most lavish of the suburb's elementary schools, Taylor was completed in 1923. This building was demolished in the 1970s. (Cleveland Heights High School Alumni Foundation.)

Six

Old and New Congregations 1963–2008

These were decades of swift, tumultuous political and demographic change across the country. The emerging civil rights movement, supported by Protestant, Catholic, and Jewish leaders and bolstered by federal legislation, encouraged African Americans to move from cities to suburbs. Like earlier suburbanites, African Americans brought their churches with them and vice versa. Simultaneously by the 1970s, membership in the major Protestant denominations began to decline from the peak achieved during the 1960s.

Cleveland Heights' population had also declined. In 2000, 42 percent were African American. Several Jewish and Protestant congregations left the city, and three churches closed or merged with other congregations. Many of the congregations that stayed took on new responsibilities, including St. Paul's Episcopal Church, Fairmount Presbyterian Church, St. Ann Church, St. Louis Church, and Forest Hill Church. The Heights Area Project, sponsored by the Jewish Community Federation, and the Heights Interfaith Council also responded to the city's changing population and its changing needs.

Older houses of worship found new owners. Four became secular institutions: First Church of Christ, Scientist, Cleveland; First English Lutheran Church; Heights United Presbyterian Church; and Oheb Zedek-Taylor Road Synagogue. Most older churches and temples, however, were purchased by new congregations: Beth El-The Heights Synagogue, Greater Peace Missionary Baptist Church, Christ Our Redeemer African Methodist Episcopal Church, New Spirit Revival Center, New Community Bible Fellowship, Mount Olive Lutheran Church, Straightway Bible Fellowship, Central Bible Baptist Church. Other new congregations, like those who preceded them, borrowed, adapted, or shared space, including Edgehill Community Church, Unity Center Church, and Cleveland Heights Church. Some old churches rebuilt or built anew, such as St. Alban Episcopal Church and Church of the Saviour. There were other significant new faces. Women, who have filled the pews and coffers of churches for decades, now fill the pulpits of some congregations, including Forest Hill Church, New Spirit Revival Center, Church of the Redeemer United Methodist, and Disciples Christian Church.

As in the past, Cleveland Heights congregations have both encouraged the new—residents, members, thinking, and responsibilities—and cherished the old, preserving traditions and rituals for their members as well as the dignity and beauty of the community's houses of worship and its neighborhoods.

DR. MARTIN LUTHER KING JR. AT ST. PAUL'S EPISCOPAL CHURCH, 1963. The leader of the national civil rights movement spoke to an overflow crowd at the church on May 14, 1963. Cleveland Heights residents were well aware that their community was on the verge of significant racial change. Cleveland Heights' African American population was very small, just 1 percent of the city's residents in 1960 and 2 percent in 1970. But even these small numbers provoked racial conflict and violence, including vandalism, arson, and one racially motivated murder. Religious congregations played a leading role in easing racial tensions and pursuing racial justice. (Western Reserve Historical Society.)

ST. ANN CHURCH FIRST COMMUNION DAY, 1977. The inclusion of African Americans in their churches made members sensitive to racial issues. In 1972, members of the St. Ann Social Action Committee discovered significant racial discrimination and racial steering by local realtors. Out of this research, called the St. Ann Audit, grew the Heights Community Congress. The congress's first members were Protestant, Catholic, and Jewish congregations; its goal remains a racially balanced community. (Karen Laborde.)

MASS AT ST. LOUIS CHURCH, 1998. Fr. Len Zamborsky celebrated this mass that acknowledged both the congregation's racially integrated membership and the changes in the liturgy after the Second Vatican Council promoted broader participation by laypersons. (St. Louis Church.)

JEWISH FESTIVAL ON THE HEIGHTS, 1981. The festival was sponsored by the Heights Area Project, established in 1972 by the Jewish Community Federation, which, like the Heights Community Congress, wanted to keep Cleveland Heights a racially integrated community. Because of the significant financial investment that the Jewish community had made in Cleveland Heights, for example, the Jewish Community Center, the project encouraged Jewish families and institutions to move to or stay in the community. Despite the project's efforts to keep Jews in the "Heights area where yesterday and today meet," Conservative and Orthodox congregations continued their exodus to farther eastern suburbs. (Western Reserve Historical Society.)

HEIGHTS EMERGENCY FOOD CENTER. This center at Disciples Christian Church was opened in 1981 by the Heights Interfaith Council, an organization of religious congregations, schools, and other community organizations established in 1975. The council's goal is to sustain "an economically and racially diverse community." This food center, completely staffed by volunteers like Hazel Haffner and aided by public and private funds, served almost 10,000 low-income persons in 2007. (Author's collection.)

FOREST HILL CHURCH MISSION PROJECT. Its predecessor, Cleveland Heights Presbyterian Church, sought to save souls; Forest Hill Church also sought to save homes. In 1972, the congregation formed the Forest Hill Housing Corporation, whose goal was to preserve and rehabilitate Cleveland Heights housing. The corporation, now the Home Repair Resource Center, provides low-interest loans, financial counseling, and workshops for homeowners as well as the manpower of volunteers. (Home Repair Resource Center.)

OPEN DOORS AT ST. PAUL'S EPISCOPAL CHURCH. This program began at St. Paul's in 1992 as a drop-in program for Roxboro Middle School students who lingered at the church on their way home from school. Open Doors now operates five days a week after school. Volunteers and staff provide educational and enrichment services to children and families. Initially funded only by the church, Open Doors is now incorporated as an independent nonprofit organization that receives private and public funds. The program served more than 100 children in 2006; 85 percent were African American. In 2005, Open Doors opened a second site at Fairmount Presbyterian Church across the street. (Open Doors.)

NOTTINGHAM SPIRK AND DESIGN. Some former houses of worship have found new uses. In 2002, the First Church of Christ, Scientist, Cleveland, on Overlook Road sold its magnificent 1929 building (see page 67) to this design firm, which has preserved the entire exterior and adapted the interior for its own use. (James W. Garrett IV.)

BROWNSTONES AT DERBYSHIRE. The congregation of the First English Lutheran Church disbanded in 2002 and sold its handsome Gothic building on Euclid Heights Boulevard (see page 69) to a developer who turned it into condominiums but maintained the church's original entrance and its trademark red doors. (Author's collection.)

HEIGHTS YOUTH CLUB. Housed in the former Heights United Presbyterian Church (see page 39), the club provides education and recreation programs after school and during the summer. The club is affiliated with the national Boys and Girls Clubs of America. (Author's collection.)

GREATER HEIGHTS ACADEMY. Oheb Zedek-Taylor Road Synagogue (see page 58) still holds services at this site, but the building is now owned by this charter school that occupies the large education wing constructed by the synagogue. (Author's collection.)

UNITARIAN UNIVERSALIST SOCIETY OF CLEVELAND. When congregations moved or disbanded, most sold their former houses of worship to other religious organizations. This congregation bought the former home of Marmarosher Shul on Lancashire Road in 1975 (see page 61). The Unitarian Universalist lamp is superimposed on the Jewish Star of David over the front door. (Author's collection.)

GREATER PEACE MISSIONARY BAPTIST CHURCH. The first African American congregation to move into Cleveland Heights purchased this building at Fairmount Boulevard and Taylor Road in 1976 from the Church of the Blessed Hope (see page 91). This photograph was taken at its opening worship service. (Greater Peace Missionary Baptist Church.)

Christ Our Redeemer African Methodist Episcopal Church. In 1982, the congregation bought this building from the Church of the Brethren, which had occupied it since 1927. This is the oldest religious structure in Cleveland Heights, built in 1904 for the Heights Methodist Episcopal Church, now Church of the Saviour (see page 12). (Author's collection.)

Christ Our Redeemer African Methodist Episcopal Church Sanctuary. The sanctuary, like the building's exterior, remains essentially unchanged. The congregation kept the memorial stained-glass windows and organ (see page 13) and maintained the simplicity of the original sanctuary. (City of Cleveland Heights.)

THE NEW SPIRIT REVIVAL CENTER. This building, designed for B'nai Jeshurun congregation by Charles Greco (see page 51), was sold to a nonprofit corporation, the Civic, when the Jewish congregation moved to Pepper Pike in 1980. In 2001, the corporation sold the building to the New Spirit Revival Center, a nondenominational African American congregation. Like the Greater Peace Missionary Baptist and Christ Our Redeemer African Methodist Episcopal Churches, this congregation represents the growing African American presence in Cleveland Heights. (New Spirit Revival Center.)

NEW SPIRIT REVIVAL CENTER SANCTUARY. The congregation has done significant remodeling and refurbishing of this vast, sprawling 1924 structure. An example is this dramatic new sanctuary, which has been adapted for Christian worship services. (New Spirit Revival Center.)

CONGREGATION BETH EL, 1998. As other Jewish congregations were leaving Cleveland Heights, Congregation Beth El moved in. The photograph pictures the traditional march of congregation members and their Torah from their old home on Chagrin Boulevard in Shaker Heights near the Jewish Mount Pleasant–Kinsman neighborhood to their new home at the Jewish Community Center. Their route took them along Taylor Road, the site of many former and current Jewish institutions. The congregation describes itself as "traditional/egalitarian." (David Kazdan.)

CONGREGATION BETH EL-THE HEIGHTS SYNAGOGUE, 2003. In 2000, Congregation Beth El merged with a group from Congregation Beth Am that wanted to stay in the Heights after its synagogue moved. The merged congregation became Beth El-The Heights Synagogue. When the Jewish Community Center planned to close, the congregation again decided stay in Cleveland Heights and again marched their Torah to their new synagogue. (David Kazdan.)

CONGREGATION BETH EL-THE HEIGHTS SYNAGOGUE, 2007. This building was originally owned by Messiah Lutheran Church. It was purchased by Sinai Synagogue in 1953 and by Congregation Beth El-The Heights Synagogue a half century later. The building's newest owners removed the Colonial entrance added in the 1950s, restoring the building to its original Gothic appearance. (Author's collection.)

CENTRAL BIBLE BAPTIST CHURCH. The congregation purchased this one-story brick building on Noble Road in 1993. It was the former home of Gracemont Gospel Chapel, which was completed in 1952 in the then-popular Colonial style that fit comfortably with its neighbors. (James W. Garrett IV.)

NEW COMMUNITY BIBLE FELLOWSHIP. Home first to Trinity Congregational Church (see page 43) and then to the Community Temple-Beth Am (see page 57), the building became the house of worship of this primarily African American congregation in 2000. The fellowship, like the New Spirit Revival Center, is nondenominational. (James W. Garrett IV.)

MOUNT OLIVE LUTHERAN CHURCH. This American Colonial church—brick with white columns and a tall steeple—on Noble Road was built for Gethsemane Lutheran Church, a congregation founded in 1922 that probably worshipped first in the brick chapel behind this building. Mount Olive Lutheran Church purchased the building in 1975. (James W. Garrett IV.)

STRAIGHTWAY BIBLE FELLOWSHIP. Since its founding in 1992, the nondenominational congregation has worshipped in this brick chapel directly behind Mount Olive Lutheran Church on Noble Road, probably the original home of Gethsemane Lutheran Church. (Author's collection.)

Community of Living Hope United Methodist Church. This Gothic Revival church on Caledonia Avenue was built in 1926 for the Church of the Cross, a Methodist congregation with German origins. The architect was H. W. Maurer, who also designed several distinguished churches in Cleveland as well as some Cleveland Heights homes. In 1982, the congregation received its first African American pastor and, in the 1990s, assumed its current name. (City of Cleveland Heights.)

Community of Living Hope Sanctuary. The simple sanctuary is distinguished by its Gothic windows, vaulted ceiling, and abstract crucifix. The congregation now worships with Windermere United Methodist Church in East Cleveland. As of 2008, the building was for sale. (City of Cleveland Heights.)

ST. ALBAN EPISCOPAL CHURCH/EDGEHILL COMMUNITY CHURCH. After St. Alban Episcopal Church was destroyed by fire in 1989, the congregation replaced its traditional Gothic church (see page 27) with this dramatic contemporary building that had many windows and angles. The congregation shares this facility with Edgehill Community Church, a member of the Worldwide Church of God. (St. Alban Episcopal Church.)

ST. ALBAN/ EDGEHILL COMMUNITY CHURCH SANCTUARY. Although the exterior is dramatically different, the sanctuary with its wood pews and beamed ceilings retains the intimate feeling of the old church (see page 27). (St. Alban Episcopal Church.)

CLEVELAND HEIGHTS CHURCH. This nondenominational congregation was founded in 2005, meeting first at the Alcazar Hotel and then at the India Community Center on Cedar Road. Like the suburb's very first congregations, this congregation has borrowed and adapted a worship space, and like them also, its members are active proselytizers for themselves and for the community. (Cleveland Heights Community Church.)

UNITY CENTER CHURCH. This brick-and-frame building on Taylor Road near Fairmount Boulevard was built in the 1940s as an office for the East Ohio Gas Company. The congregation bought the property in 1975. (Author's collection.)

FOREST HILL CHURCH. Associate pastor Rev. Clover Beal and senior pastor Rev. John Lentz officiated at this baptism. Women have constituted the majority of church members since at least the 19th century but have become ordained ministers of the major Protestant denominations only in the last four decades. (Forest Hill Church.)

NEW SPIRIT REVIVAL CENTER. Dr. Darrell Scott and Dr. Belinda Scott founded the New Spirit Revival Center in 1994. She also founded the Women's Educational Mentoring Alliance to educate other women who desire to become ministers. (New Spirit Revival Center.)

DISCIPLES CHRISTIAN CHURCH. Rev. Kristine Eggert is senior pastor of this congregation. She and her staff are among the many women clergy of Cleveland Heights congregations. (Disciples Christian Church.)

CHURCH OF THE REDEEMER UNITED METHODIST CHURCH. Rev. Karen Burtner Graham became pastor of this congregation in July 2005. The presence of women in the pulpit is perhaps the most dramatic change experienced by Protestant and Jewish congregations in the last century. (Church of the Redeemer United Methodist.)

CLEVELAND HEIGHTS CITY HALL. In 1986, the City of Cleveland Heights moved its city hall from its historic location at Mayfield and Superior Roads east on Mayfield to a site adjoining Severance Town Center. The replacement of the 1924 city hall that had architectural references to an Anglo-American past (see page 39) with this contemporary structure represents a changed Cleveland Heights, whose residents come from all racial, ethnic, and class backgrounds. The old city hall was within an easy walk of two churches, Methodist and Presbyterian. The new city hall is within an easy walk of many houses of worship. Today they are Protestant, Jewish, Catholic, and nondenominational. (Author's collection.)

CHURCH OF THE SAVIOUR'S NEWEST ADDITION. The history of this congregation, the oldest in Cleveland Heights, also tells the story of this community. As Fairmount/Heights Methodist Episcopal Church, the congregation arrived in 1875 on a mission to save the heathens of this rural village in East Cleveland Township. By the 1920s, the congregation became the affluent Church of the Saviour, just as the village became a prosperous suburb. Like Cleveland Heights, the church has continued to adapt to the present. This spacious new addition houses a contemporary worship space but retains the Gothic look of the congregation's earlier buildings. Although much grander, the stone addition's pointed windows and roof are reminiscent of the congregation's first home of its own, the very modest frame building to the south of the Superior Schoolhouse (see page 11). (Author's collection.)

CONNECTING THE PRESENT AND THE PAST. Forest Hill Church, formerly Cleveland Heights Presbyterian Church, one of Cleveland Heights' oldest congregations, celebrated its centennial in 2003 with this walk through Cumberland Park, once the vineyards of J. M. Preyer. The walk took the congregation from its current home on Monticello Boulevard and Lee Road, past its site at Mayfield and Preyer Roads at the end of the park, to its early home at the Superior Schoolhouse (now the Cleveland Heights Historical Center). Although the congregation has changed significantly over the century, it has remained very close to its beginnings. This journey also celebrated the importance of the past to the present and the future of Cleveland Heights congregations. (Forest Hill Church.)

BIBLIOGRAPHY

Across the Years, the Towers Rise. Cleveland Heights, OH: Church of the Saviour, 1950.

Bayless, Frances B. *A Jubilee of Christian Service Past and Future*. Cleveland Heights, OH: Fairmount Presbyterian Church, 1992.

Bellamy, John Stark. *Angels on the Heights: A History of St. Ann's Parish Cleveland Heights, Ohio, 1915–1990*. Cleveland Heights, OH: St. Ann Church, 1990.

Church of Christ of Forest Hill. Twentieth Anniversary Celebration, 1960–1980. Cleveland Heights, OH: Church of Christ of Forest Hill, 1980.

Euclid Avenue Christian Church: The First 150 Years, 1843–1993. Cleveland Heights, OH: Euclid Avenue Christian Church, 1993.

50th Anniversary Noble Road Presbyterian Church, 1921–1971.

Golden Jubilee: The Catholic Community of St. Louis. Barberton, OH.

Hanson, Rev. Robert. *The First English Lutheran Church, 1881–1981 Centennial Year*. Cleveland Heights, OH.

Harris, Mary Emma. *A Century of Christian Progress: Church of the Master Baptist, 1859–1959*. Cleveland Heights, OH: Church of the Master, 1959.

Harris, Mary Emma and Ruth Mills Robinson. *The Proud Heritage of Cleveland Heights, Ohio*. Oberlin, OH: Oberlin Printing Company, 1966.

In the Beginning: The History of Forest Hill Church. Cleveland Heights, OH: Forest Hill Church, 1993.

Jarvis, F. Washington. *St. Paul's, Cleveland, 1846–1968*. Cleveland Heights, OH: St. Paul Episcopal Church, 1967.

Leedy, Roy B. *The Evangelical Church in Ohio*. Cleveland, OH: The Ohio Conference of the Evangelical United Brethren Church, 1959.

Marsden, George M. *Religion and American Culture*. New York: Harcourt Brace Jovanovich, 1990.

Morton, Marian J. *Cleveland Heights: The Making of an Urban Suburb*. Charleston, SC; Arcadia Publishing, 2002.

Rodgers, Robert C., Eleanor W. Richardson, and Gordon D. Rowe. *Church of the Saviour: A Faith-Filled Landmark*. Cleveland Heights, OH: Church of the Saviour, 2001.

Williams, Peter W. *America's Religions: Traditions and Cultures*. New York: MacMillan Publishing Company, 1990.

Women's Civic Club of Cleveland Heights, MSS 3641. Cleveland, OH: Western Reserve Historical Society.

INDEX